SEA HISTORY's GUIDE TO
American and Canadian
MARITIME MUSEUMS

Compiled and Edited by Joseph M. Stanford

ADVISORY COMMITTEE

MICHAEL NAAB, CHAIRMAN
NORMAN J. BROUWER
JOHN S. CARTER
HAROLD D. HUYCKE
KARL KORTUM

SEA HISTORY PRESS
Croton-on-Hudson

ACKNOWLEDGEMENTS: Heartfelt thanks are owed to museum directors and curators across America and Canada who make possible everything reported in these pages and who answered every question we put to them with enthusiastic interest in the development of this guide. Particular thanks go to the members of the Advisory Committee who patiently reviewed the work for accuracy: Chairman, Michael Naab, Director of Maritime Preservation, National Trust for Historic Preservation; Norman J. Brouwer, Curator of Ships, South Street Seaport Museum, New York; John S. Carter, Director of the Philadelphia Maritime Museum and Past President, Council of American Maritime Museums; Captain Harold D. Huycke, ship surveyor and maritime historian, of Seattle; and Karl Kortum, Chief Curator of the San Francisco Maritime National Historic Park and Chairman Emeritus of the National Maritime Historical Society.

And to the members and supporters of the National Maritime Historical Society, notably Texaco Inc., whose generous support made it possible to offer this guide at an affordable price.

Let us invite you to join our Society, reader, and keep in touch. Membership is $25 made out to NMHS at PO Box 646, Croton-on-Hudson NY 10520. Members receive the quarterly magazine *Sea History*, discounts on publications and notice of meetings. In the words of the old song, "There's a hearty welcome waiting. . . ."

Cover photograph by John Kortum.

Contents

FOREWORD

Why Maritime Culture is Important to Our Comprehension of Our National Experience

by John S. Carter
Director, Philadelphia Maritime Museum
Past President, Council of American Maritime Museums
Vice President, International Congress of Maritime Museums

In 1799 a group of Salem, Massachusetts, sea captains formed the East India Marine Society in their far-trading port city. Acceptance in this exclusive group was relatively easy by eighteenth century New England standards; one just had to be a mariner and had to have sailed around the Cape of Good Hope at the southern tip of Africa or Cape Horn, the southernmost point of South America—such long voyages were regularly accomplished by a goodly number of Salem's captains and supercargoes. One important aspect of the Society was a cabinet containing curiosities brought back by members from their worldwide travels. And so America's first "mariner's museum" was started nearly two hundred years ago.

Maritime museums have progressed a long way since this first narrowly based beginning in late eighteenth-century Salem, as this *Sea History's Guide to American and Canadian Maritime Museums* will amply attest. Diverse in collections and activities and thronged by visitors in all walks of life, our maritime history museums today offer a broad range of experiences geared to all members of the family. Recreation-based learning experience with hands-on programs in maritime crafts, sailing and related activities now augment the rich collections of historical artifacts gathered by our nation's maritime museums. These organizations present opportunities as diverse as walking the deck of a whaling vessel to going below on a submarine to seeing the pots and pans and sailmaker's tools of people who sailed before our time—the commonplace "things" of history that have made the United States what it is today.

In today's world of superhighways spanning the land under skies criss-crossed by the vapor trails of jetliners, it is sometimes hard to imagine the role played by slow-moving sailing ships, splashing paddlewheel steamers and mule-drawn canal boats in building the nation. But it is a fact that waterborne commerce and the entrepreneurship of the American merchant marine brought the United States to the forefront among nations. Within the country the coastal waterways, rivers and canals were the nation's highways. The early republic crowded close by the shore and it was to the water that our villages, towns and cities faced, both literally and figuratively.

Our maritime museums, great and small, bring these scenes to life for us. They help us understand why today a majority of America's great cities are still port cities and the coast still holds an allure for all of us. While the American merchant marine has seen great erosion over the years, the United States still depends on waterborne commerce and the American public is still drawn to the waterfront as a place to work and to pursue recreational activities. The nation's maritime museums help preserve that vital link and help us to gain an understanding of why maritime culture is important to our comprehension of our national experience.

Maritime museums are as diverse as the waterways that encircle and permeate our geography. Some organizations flourish in important and long-standing oceanport cities such as New York and San Francisco, while others can be found along our lakes and rivers or in rural coastal areas where fishing and local trade was important. An important common denominator in all of the organizations in this guide is that they all seek to educate and enlighten the public about our universal maritime experience. These museums, some old, some relatively new, all work together as a community, much like the ships they seek to interpret. There are strong linkages between them that are strengthening as the community evolves in developing purpose and growing outreach.

Frankly, this is an exciting time to visit these museums, because nearly all of them have made major advances in their programs, galleries and interpretations in recent years. They offer a multi-dimensional experience that goes as deeply as the visitor wishes to go. A first-time visitor might be content to browse through collections of paintings, ship models and traditional sailor's gear. In subsequent visits he or she (or they) might want to go further—join the museum to share in evening lectures and craft demonstrations, or enroll in a boatbuilding course, or pursue studies in the great resource offered by museum libraries with their ever-helpful staff.

The maritime museum of today has become first and foremost an education center that represents a creative experience for its visitors. These museums invite you to participate in a "real" experience, not one that is manufactured as in a popular theme park or merely passive and "entertaining" as in a TV show. Each of these places is unique and yet they all form the community that represents our diverse maritime heritage. We invite each of you to sample the rich diversity that makes up this unique and endlessly challenging American experience.

INTRODUCTION

Wherever Americans have lived their lives in close interaction with the water, there seems to be a museum or historical society dedicated to preserving and promoting that history—from tiny canal towns hundreds of miles from the sea to great coastal cities built upon ocean trade. We hope this guide will encourage wider exploration into our maritime heritage, and that our readers will become more involved in the heritage. All museums welcome participation, whether it is becoming a member, volunteering help or attending special events.

In designing the guide, we have striven to include as much information as possible, while keeping the format simple, concise, low-priced and readily updatable. The museums are grouped by state, within which the entries are arranged by size. In each size category, entries are alphabetized by name (not by town). As much as possible, we have tried to keep the original language provided by the museums themselves, and, with a few exceptions, all the information presented here has been verified by the museums. But changes are taking place continually—exhibits are added, hours change and programs differ from season to season. Especially when travelling, phoning ahead can assure that you see what you are planning to (ships occasionally go into drydock) and that you are aware of any special demonstrations or programs.

This guide is by no means a closed statement on the community of maritime museums. This is a first edition, the beginning of what we like to think of as an ongoing process in a growing and constantly changing field. We welcome your comments and suggestions for future editions.

—JMS

ALABAMA

Fort Morgan State Historic Park, County Route 180, Mobile Point AL 36542, tel (205) 540-7125. Site of the famous Civil War battle at Mobile Bay, this small museum tells the fort's history and displays Civil War artifacts of Union and Confederate ships. Open year round, Mon-Fri 8am-9pm; Sat & Sun 9-5. Adults $2, Children $1.

USS *Alabama* Battleship Commission & Submarine *Drum*, PO Box 65, Mobile AL 36601, tel (205) 433-2703. The 680-ft, 43,500-ton *Alabama* (BB 60), launched 1942, served in both the Atlantic and Pacific. The *Drum* (SS 228) served in the Pacific. Both are open for self-guided tours. Aircraft are also on display in the park. Open year round. Adults $5, Children $2.50.

ALASKA

Fairbanks Historical Preservation Foundation, 755 Eighth Ave., Fairbanks AK 99701, tel (907) 456-8848. The sternwheel riverboat *Nenana* undergoing restoration. Call for information.

CALIFORNIA, San Francisco
San Francisco Maritime National Historical Park

To preserve and interpret the history and achievements of seafaring Americans and of the nation's maritime heritage, especially on the Pacific Coast.

The Historical Park, conceived by Karl Kortum in 1949, recounts the saga of the people and ships that helped shape the development of the Pacific Coast, focusing on the story of San Francisco's growth into a world-class city—a city literally built on the hulls of the vessels which brought its founders to the Gold Rush. In 1983 the San Francisco Maritime Museum (opened in 1951) and its progeny, the separately operated San Francisco State Maritime Historic Park at Hyde Street Pier were consolidated into the Maritime Unit of the Golden Gate National Recreation Area. In 1988 Congress established the Museum and Hyde Street Pier ships as a separate National Park.

The Park spans 35 acres of the city's historic waterfront adjacent to Fisherman's Wharf. Its nine buildings, including a 1912 Army warehouse, 1907 cannery, and a 1939 casino, total over 114,000 sq ft, with about 50,000 used for exhibits. With an annual budget of $2.8 million, the Park has about 100 full- and part-time employees, 765 members, and 40 volunteers.

The Park's tremendous collection contains over 5,000 archaeological pieces (most from the recently uncovered Gold Rush ship *Niantic*), 120,000 ship plans, 250,000 photographs, 1,600 pieces of artwork, and another 20,000+ general historical artifacts. While only a fraction of the collection is on display at one time, the majority is accessible through three research collections in Fort Mason Center: The J. Porter Shaw Library, which houses over 12,000 volumes as well as more than 300 oral history interviews, periodicals and ephemeral material; the Historic Documents Department, which manages collections of archives, manuscripts, log books, ship plans and photographs; and the Collections Management Department, which houses the main body of maritime artifacts and fine arts which may be viewed for research by appointment.

Exhibits: The exhibits in the museum building—located just across from Ghirardelli Square—span more than a century of West Coast seafaring history, from the 1840s to the present. Parts of original San Francisco Bay vessels and numerous ship models are displayed on the main floor. The Steamship Gallery, also on the main floor, offers a comprehensive display of the technology and history of steamships on the West Coast. Upstairs, exhibits of artifacts and photographs recall the days of the California Gold Rush, Cape Horners and whaling. Here visitors experience the lives of the men and women who built, supplied, and sailed ships when waterways were still the major means of transportation. Also on the second floor is the Harmon Gallery, which features thematic displays on a rotating basis. There are also exhibits aboard ships and on the pier.

Vessels: The historic ship collection is a major highlight of the Park. Berthed at the Hyde Street Pier are the 1886 square-rigged *Balclutha*, which carried coal, whiskey and window glass, etc. from Europe and left with California grain; 1890 sidewheeler *Eureka*, once the world's largest passenger ferry; 1891 San Francisco Bay scow schooner *Alma*, which transported bulk cargoes of lumber, hay and other products until highways and more efficient tranportation routes

The *Balclutha, C.A. Thayer* and *Wapama* at the Hyde Street Pier.

phased her out; 1895 schooner *C.A. Thayer*, the last old-time commercial sailing vessel to operate from an American West Coast port; 1907 steam tug *Hercules*, which hauled log rafts down the West Coast to lumber mills and towed sailing ships out to sea; and the 1914 British-built paddle tug *Eppleton Hall*. Also at the Pier is a working small-boat shop. The Liberty ship *Jeremiah O'Brien*, operated by the National Liberty Ship Memorial, is docked nearby at Pier 3, Fort Mason, and the World War II submarine *Pampanito*, operated by the National Maritime Museum Association, is berthed at Pier 45. The 1915 steam schooner *Wapama* can be viewed in Sausalito at the Bay Model Visitor Center.

Programs, Activities & Events: A team of docents and park rangers run an educational program designed to develop a greater understanding and appreciation of Pacific Coast maritime history. This includes ship and museum tours, films, classes, Christmas programs, chantey sings, and special events. An educational program for children that includes overnight and in-school workshops is designed to help students understand the life of a sailor and see themselves as part of history. Frequently scheduled events include concerts, tours, and new exhibit openings. Yearly programs and events include small boat classes, a small craft regatta, and the Festival of the Sea.

Location: The Park extends from the foot of Hyde Street to Laguna Street on San Francisco Bay, adjacent to Fisherman's Wharf. The museum building is at the foot of Polk Street across from Ghirardelli Square.

Schedule: Museum building open May-Oct, Wed-Sun, 10am-6pm, November-April, Wed-Sun, 10am-5pm. Other facilities' schedules vary.

Admission: All facilities free exept Hyde St. Pier: Adults $2, Children and Seniors free.

San Francisco Maritime National Historical Park

Membership
Gift Shop
Picnic Area
Limited Parking

Fort Mason, Building 201
San Francisco CA 94123
(415) 556-3002
William G. Thomas, Superintendent

3

CALIFORNIA, San Pedro
Los Angeles Maritime Museum

To provide a window to the seafaring past, specifically the history and development of the Port of Los Angeles as one of America's busiest seaports.

The 75,000 square-foot former San Pedro ferry terminal is home to the Los Angeles Maritime Museum. Founded in 1980—as part of a city-sponsored revitalization effort, which has created a renaissance in the waterfront communities of WORLDPORT LA—the museum is owned and operated by the City of Los Angeles Harbor and Recreation/Parks Departments.

Exhibits, Programs & Events: Situated virtually in the heart of Los Angeles Harbor, the museum devotes much attention to the 150-year history of San Pedro and the growth of the Port of Los Angeles. Photographs and artifacts from the harbor help tell the story of this extensive development. An amateur radio station brings it into the present by allowing visitors to hear radio communications of the modern tugs, barges, liners, and supertankers plying the waters just outside. The scope of presentation is broad, though, accommodating all of California's maritime history and offering the visitor a taste of such topics as naval history, the merchant marine, the whaling industry, maritime arts and crafts, and nautical lore. Among the more notable exhibits are a hands-on knotting display, a life-size recreated flying bridge of USS *Los Angeles*, and figureheads. The museum's ship model collection is one of the world's largest, comprised of over 700 models, including a recreation of the entire Great White Fleet, an 18-foot cut-away *Titanic*, and a 22-foot cruise-liner model used in the 1972 film "The Poseidon Adventure." Public programs made available by the Museum include classes in small boat handling, ship model building, the art of scrimshaw, celestial navigation, and ocean vessel handling. Volunteer programs and special events are hosted at the museum throughout the year. These include tall ship visits, festivals, and cooperative activities with community arts and historical organizations.

Location: On the waterfront in San Pedro, next to Ports O' Call Village.
Schedule: Year round, Tuesday-Sunday 10am-5pm.
Admission: Free.

Gift shop
Free Parking
Research Library

Los Angeles Maritime Museum
Foot of Sixth Street, Berth 84
San Pedro CA 90731
(213) 548-7618
William Lee, PhD, Director

San Diego Maritime Museum

To function as a non-profit public institution that exhibits maritime artifacts and a research library on three floating historic vessels and provides supporting programs and publications depicting San Diego's rich maritime heritage in the context of the West Coast and the Pacific Rim.

The Museum Association was founded in 1927 to save the bark *Star of India*, and has since grown into three fully-restored ships moored along San Diego's Embarcadero. Offices and an 8,000-volume, 8,000-photograph library are located on the ferryboat *Berkeley*. The museum has 35 employees, 1,500 members and an $802,000 annual budget.

Exhibits & Vessels: The 289-foot, 1,945-ton ferryboat *Berkeley*, built in 1898 to carry passengers between Oakland and San Francisco, houses most of the museum's exhibits, a ship model shop, and a research library. Exhibits cover naval history, the merchant marine, ferryboats of San Diego Bay, West Coast merchant sail, Coast Guard operations in the Pacific, steam engines, San Diego fishing industry, yachting, and West Coast whaling. The library holds large collections of rare 18th and 19th century books, 19th century ships' logs, photographs, plans, and charts. *Berkeley*, herself, is quite a display too, with finely restored woodwork, stained glass, and an operating engine.

Built on the Isle of Man in 1863 as a full-rigged merchant ship, *Star of India* (originally *Euterpe*) served many purposes, carrying general cargo between England and India, emigrants from England to Australia, and general cargo between North America, Hawaii and Australia. She sailed around the world 21 times in her 60-year career. Exhibits, restored cabins, and the occasional craft demonstration on board relate many facets of sailing ship life.

Medea, one of the few remaining large steam yachts, has been fully restored to her pre-WWI elegance and frequently makes tours of San Diego Bay.

Programs & Events: The Museum conducts a year-round sail training program aboard *Star of India*, culminating in a voyage every three years. There are also members' programs which present various aspects of maritime history, and a docent training program. The Museum's speakers' bureau gives talks on museum-related topics to community groups and schools.

Location: Vessels are moored along North Harbor Drive at the foot of Ash Street in downtown San Diego on the Embarcadero.

Schedule: Year round, every day 9am-8pm.

Admission: Adults $5, Youths (13-17) $4, Children (6-12) $1.25, Children under 6 free, Seniors $4, Families $10, Group rates available.

Membership
Gift shop
Paid parking

Maritime Museum Association of San Diego
1306 N. Harbor Drive
San Diego CA 92101
(619) 234-9153
Kenneth Franke, Director

CALIFORNIA, Monterey
Allen Knight Maritime Museum

To collect, preserve, and display artifacts, artwork, and documents pertaining to the maritime history of California and Monterey, with emphasis on the whaling and fishing industries.

Founded in 1971 around the private collection of Allen Knight, the Museum has about 1,500 square feet of exhibit space, 2,500 books, 14,000 photos and 100 paintings.

Exhibits consist mainly of a large collection of ship models, photographs, and various shipboard implements. The ship models represent a wide range of vessels from California's history, including the first Spanish ships on the West Coast and the small open fishing boats of the region. The rest of the collection, which includes a first-order fresnel lens, attends strongly to Monterey history, and especially to the brief history of its whaling industry in the late 19th century, and the successful, but also short-lived, regional fishing industry.

Schedule: Year round, Tues-Fri 1-4pm, Sat-Sun 2-4pm. **Admission:** Free.

Allen Knight Maritime Museum, 550 Calle Principal, PO Box 805
Monterey CA 93942 (408) 375-2553 Donna Penwell, Director

CALIFORNIA, Dana Point
Nautical Heritage Museum

To provide in-depth character-building programs for youth, and to educate the public about our maritime heritage and marine environment.

Established in 1981, the Museum offers a 3,000-square foot maritime display area, sea education training aboard its topsail schooner *Californian*, advanced sailing on a 1913 Q boat, and a Sea Explorer Post, all on a privately financed annual budget of $675,000.

Exhibits & Vessels: Displays include ship models, a scrimshaw collection, marine art and maritime artifacts. Historic documents include letters and ships' papers signed by George Washington, Isaac Hull, Lord Nelson, etc. The 145-foot Revenue cutter *Californian* serves as a year-round sail training vessel for youth and some adults and is California's "Official Tallship Ambassador." She is flagship of "Coast-Link 90," a statewide coastal awareness/environmental program and is active in coastal maritime events throughout the year. She offers half day to eleven day cruises.

Schedule: Museum: Year round, Tues-Sat 10am-4pm. *Californian* is at sea 300 days a year; contact Museum for schedule and costs. **Admission:** Free.

Nautical Heritage Museum, 24532 Del Prado, Dana Point CA 92629
(714) 661-1001 Steve Christman, Director

Treasure Island Museum

To interpret the history of the three sea services in the Pacific from 1813 to the present, and the history of Treasure Island.

Treasure Island is located in the middle of San Francisco Bay, accessed by the Bay Bridge. There, the former headquarters of the 1939 World's Fair is home to the Treasure Island Museum. Founded in 1975 as a Bicentennial project, the museum has 11,000 square feet of exhibit space, a 1,500-volume library, 5 employees and 150 members.

Exhibits: A 251-foot long mural and exhibit presents the sea services (Navy, Marine Corps, Coast Guard) in the Pacific. Using models, artifacts, paintings, photographs, prints, interactive materials and audio/visual aids, the museum documents the history of the services, Treasure Island's history, the Golden Gate International Exposition, the San Francisco-Oakland Bay Bridge, lighthouses and lightships, and the brief history of the Pan Am China Clipper flying boats. Also, visitors can enjoy a spectacular view of San Francisco, the Bay and its bridges.

Schedule: Year round, every day 10am-3:30pm. **Admission:** Free.

Treasure Island Museum
Building One, Treasure Island, San Francisco CA 94130-5000
(415) 395-5067   Edward Von Der Porten, Director

CALIFORNIA

Battery Point Lighthouse, Foot of A Street, Crescent City CA; mailing addr: Del Corte County Historical Society, 577 H. St., Crescent City Ca 95531, tel (707) 464-3089. The 1856 lighthouse contains a small museum and is open for tours Apr-Sept, Wed-Sun 10-4. Adults $1.50, Children under 12 50¢.

Cabrillo National Monument, PO Box 6670, San Diego CA 92166, tel (619) 557-5450. Located in a 144-acre park, the monument commemorates Juan Rodriguez Cabrillo's exploration of the West Coast in 1542. It also presents and interprets the cultural and natural resources of the park. Call for hours.

CEC/Seabee Museum, Port Hueneme CA 93043, tel (805) 982-5163. Established in 1947 as a memorial to the US Navy's Civil Engineer Corps and the Naval Construction Force (Seabees), the museum contains weapons, paintings, models, dioramas and personal memorabilia. Open year round, every day, Mon-Fri 8-5, Sat 9-4, Sun 12:30-4:30. Admission free.

***China* Cabin**, 52 Beach Rd. (near Tiburon Blvd.), Belvedere Cove, Tiburon CA 94920, tel (415) 435-1853. The ornately finished social saloon and two officers' cabins from William Webb's SS *China* of 1867 are fully restored and open to the public. A display of artifacts, documents and photos is planned. Open year round, daily, Mon-Fri 8-5, Sat 9-4:30, Sun 12:30-4:30. Or by appointment. Admission during regular hours is free.

CALIFORNIA

Clark Memorial Museum, Third and E Streets, Eureka CA 95501, tel (707) 443-1947. The museum has a small but interesting maritime collection featuring local craft, photos and ship models. Open year round except national holidays, Tues-Sat 10-4. Admission by donation.

East Brother's Light Station, 117 Park Pl., Point Richmond CA 94801, tel (415) 236-7435. Operates and maintains facilities on East Brother's Island. Call for hours.

Humboldt Bay Museum, 1410 Second, Eureka CA 95501, tel (707) 444-9440. Paintings, ship models, photos and artifacts tell the story of this historic port. The 1910 diesel launch *Madaket* is on display. Open year round, daily 11-4. Adults $1, Children 50¢.

Marinship 1942-1945, Bay Model Visitor Center, 2100 Bridgeway, Sausalito CA 94965, tel (415) 322-3871. This small museum relates the effort that built 93 tankers and Liberty ships during the war years. Open all year, Tues-Sat 9-4. Open Sundays summer only. Admission is free.

Queen Mary, Pier J, PO Box 8, Long Beach CA 90801, tel (213) 435-4747. Cunard's 81,000-ton luxury liner, now converted to a hotel, is open for public tours year round, Mon-Fri 10-4, Sat-Sun 9:30-4:30. Adults $10.95, Children (5-11) $6.95.

SS *Lane Victory*, US Merchant Marine Veterans of WW II, PO Box 629, Berth 52, Outer Harbor, San Pedro CA 90731. This Victory ship was built during the closing years of WWII. She remains virtually unaltered from her wartime appearance and is under restoration. She is dedicated as a memorial to America's merchant mariners of WWII and is soon to be designated a National Historic Landmark. There are special events, a volunteer program and monthly publication.

Vallejo Naval and Historical Museum, 734 Marin St., Vallejo CA 94590, tel (707) 643-0077. Housed in the old 1927 City Hall, the museum features local history with two galleries dedicated to naval themes relating to the nearby Mare Island naval base. Open year round, Tues-Sat 10-4:30. Adults $1, Seniors and Children 50¢.

Ventura County Maritime Museum, Channel Islands Harbor, PO Box 190, Ventura CA 93002, tel (805) 486-9867. Scheduled to open late 1990. Phone or write for information.

CONNECTICUT, Mystic
Mystic Seaport Museum

To preserve materials, artifacts, vessels and skills relating to maritime history in order to enhance man's knowledge and understanding of the sea's influence on American life.

Founded in 1929 as the Marine Historical Association, the Seaport has grown to become America's preeminent maritime museum and the biggest tourist attraction in the state of Connecticut. With a research library larger than those of many small universities (over 350,000 volumes) and what is probably the largest collection of historic watercraft in the world, Mystic is recognized worldwide not only for the broad scope and depth of its presentations but as

a major center of information regarding all facets of man's seafaring experience. The Seaport is actively involved in keeping alive Amerca's seafaring tradition through the ships, buildings, artifacts and skills of the past.

The Seaport occupies a 17-acre site on the Mystic River, a few miles up from the eastern end of Long Island Sound. The Seaport operates on a $10 million annual budget and has 20,000 members, a staff of 250 full time and 100 part time employees assisted by hundreds of volunteers. In addition to the library, there are several other collections used for reference purposes and exhibits including the Rosenfeld Collection of Photographs, which contains over 1 million images.

Exhibits: The Seaport's main exhibit, "New England and the Sea," occupies the ground floor of the Stillman Building. It chronologically explores all the major aspects of the region's maritime history, integrating artifacts, ship models, paintings, photographs and other visual aids. On the building's second floor is the main collection of ship models, scrimshaw and other mariners' handiwork. Nearby are the other main exhibit buildings which house the *Benjamin F. Packard* ship's cabin, small craft exhibit, and figureheads. There are a total of approximately 60 separate exhibits interspersed throughout the grounds.

Historic Seaport Structures: The heritage of coastal New England is very much alive in the Seaport's historic structures, which together recreate an authentic 19th century village. More than 30 buildings, many moved from surrounding areas, are maintained open to the public in their 19th century settings. Among them are several houses, a chapel, meeting house, store, bank, schoolhouse, ropewalk, sail loft, rigging loft, ship chandlery, shipsmith, hoop shop, cooperage, tavern, and many others. Most of the trades buildings are in operating condition and are frequently put to use for their original purposes. Of special interest are the planetarium which shows daily films, a lifesaving station moved from Block Island, and a 50-foot diorama of Mystic's waterfront when the town was a major shipbuilding center.

Vessels: The Museum's collection contains over 400 watercraft, representing many modes of marine transportation seen on the East Coast. Berthed at Chubb's Wharf is the Seaport's flagship, *Charles W. Morgan*, America's sole-surviving wooden whaleship. A 113-foot bark built in 1841, she sailed for more than 80 years—longer than any whaleship on record. She was retired and put

on display in South Dartmouth, Massachusetts, in 1921 and acquired by the museum in 1941. Today she is well kept, with all her original equipment intact and fully open for tours. The 111-foot iron square rigger *Joseph Conrad*, built in Copenhagen in 1882, served most of her career as a

training ship and today houses the living quarters for the Seaport's sail training program. At the Seaport's southern end is the *L. A. Dunton*, a 123-foot Gloucester fishing schooner built in 1921 in Essex, Massachusetts. SS *Sabino*, built in Maine in 1908, is one of the last coal-fired passenger steamboats operating in the United States and still takes passengers on daily tours of the river in the summer. Several smaller vessels are moored just offshore or berthed along one of the museum's many wharves. Small craft are on display in the water and in many exhibits.

Preservation Shipyard: The DuPont Preservation Shipyard at the Seaport's southern end contains a visitors gallery, the main preservation shop, a lift dock capable of hauling out the seaport's largest vessels, and the *Thames* Keel Shipbuilding Exhibit. The main shop is large enough to hold several vessels at once, and is in use every day for restoration and new boat construction. A balcony runs the length of the building, from which visitors can observe the work in progress.

Activities, Programs & Events: Daily activities include crafts demonstrations, tours, films, steamboat cruises and carriage rides. Throughout 1991 the Seaport will celebrate 150 years of the *Charles W. Morgan* with special events and exhibits. Major annual events: Yachting History Symposium (February), Lobster Festival (May), Small Craft Weekend and Sea Music Festival (June), Antique and Classic Boat Rendezvous (July), Schooner Race (September), Maritime History Symposium (November). The Seaport has classes in boatbuilding and marine sciences (jointly with Williams College), navigation and astronomy, a variety of arts and crafts, and an internship program.

Location: On Route 27 in Mystic, one mile south of I-95 exit 90.

Schedule: Open every day 9am-5pm; Winter 10am-4pm; July-Aug 9am-8pm.

Admission: Adults $14, Children (6-15) $7.75, Children 5 and under free. Reduced rates for group visits. Members free.

Membership	**Mystic Seaport Museum Inc.**
Gift Shop	PO Box 6000
Picnic Area	50 Greenmanville Avenue
Restaurants	Mystic CT 06355-0990
Cafeteria	(203) 572-0711
Free Parking	J. Revell Carr, President

CONNECTICUT, Essex
Connecticut River Museum

To collect, preserve, and interpret materials related to the Connecticut River Valley; and to explore the history of people's relation to the river by navigation, commerce and industry, maritime trades, agriculture and recreation.

At the foot of Main Street, on Essex's Steamboat Dock, the museum occupies an 1878 warehouse, along with adjacent boathouse and non-circulating research library. A waterfront park and dock are used for seasonal programs and events.

Exhibits & Vessels: The permanent exhibits feature a chronological history from the geological formation of the valley to early man, European discovery and settlement, colonial agriculture, shipbuilding, the stone trade and other river-related industries, including fisheries, steamboating, and yachting. Of special interest is the working reproduction of the first submarine, *American Turtle*, built on the river in 1775 for the American Revolution. Area archaeology and regional folklife are incorporated into the annually changing exhibits. The small craft collection includes examples of a river-built drag boat for fishing, small day sailers, and a pair of work boats housed in an 80-sq ft boat house. Museum programs include a winter lecture series, river cruises, dockside concerts and traditional vessel events.

Schedule: Year round, Tues-Sun 10-5. **Admission:** Adults $2.50, Seniors $2.

Connecticut River Museum, PO Box 261, Essex CT 06426
(203) 767-8269   Brenda Milkofsky, Director

CONNECTICUT, South Norwalk
Maritime Center at Norwalk

To further public appreciation of marine science and culture as well as the particular power and fragility of Long Island Sound.

Built in and around a 19th century factory on five acres of waterfront, the Center contains an aquarium complex, a maritime culture hall and an Imax theater.

Exhibits & Vessels: the Aquarium displays a series of tanks, beginning with the wetlands and salt marshes and proceeding in stages to the depths of the sound and the ocean beyond. In all, 175 species of marine life, including harbor seals and a 10-ft shark are on view. The Maritime Hall focuses on the sea-related culture of the area. Actual vessels include the *Hope*, a 56-ft sailing oyster sloop; a replica of the *Middlesex*, used to raid British shipping during the Revolution; the Naphtha launch *Glory Days* of 1900; and the catamaran *Patient Lady V*. The Center also runs a variety of innovative programs and expeditions.

Schedule: Year round, every day; Winter 10am-5pm; Summer 10am-6pm.
Admission: Aquarium or Imax: Adult $5.50, Seniors and Children $4.50. Combination: Adult $9.50, Seniors and Children $7.50.

The Maritime Center at Norwalk
10 North Water Street, South Norwalk CT 06854
(203) 852-0700   Vilma P. Allen, Director

Nautilus Memorial and Submarine Force Museum

To preserve, increase, and disseminate knowledge of the history and development of the US Navy's Submarine Force in specific and submarines worldwide in general.

Begun in 1955 by Electric Boat, the Submarine Force Library is today the Navy's official submarine museum. Occupying a 14,000 sq ft building opened in 1986, the Museum has a 5,000-volume reference library and comprehensive photo and document archives. *Nautilus* (SSN 571), the world's first nuclear-powered submarine and first ship to go to the North Pole, is open for public visitation. The self-guided tour includes the torpedo room, attack center, living quarters, and other spaces.

Exhibits include a full size replica of Bushnell's Revolutionary War *Turtle*, three operating periscopes, and a 50-ft scale model of a World War II *Gato* class submarine. Two mini-theatres continually show films on submarine history and operations. Scale models trace submarine development from *Holland* (SS-1) to modern Trident submarines. Other exhibits depict life on submarines. Outside are a 42-ft hull section from a Trident submarine and four midget submarines.

Schedule: Year round, closed Tuesdays. October 15-April 14, 9am-3:30pm; April 15-October 14, 9am-5pm. **Admission:** Free.

Nautilus Memorial/Submarine Force Library & Museum
Box 571, Groton CT 06349-5000
(203) 449-3174   William Galvani, Director

CONNECTICUT

Captain's Cove Seaport, 1 Bostwick Ave., Bridgeport CT 06605, tel (203) 335-1433. The central attraction is *HMS Rose*, a full-size replica of an 18th century British frigate. Seaport open year round 8-5. The *Rose* is open Apr-Oct, daily 12-5. Seaport is admission free; *Rose*: Adults $3, Children $2.

Custom House Maritime Museum, c/o New London Maritime Society, 150 Bank St., New London CT 06320, tel (203) 447-2501. This new museum is located in an 1833 US Customs House. As we go to press, the museum is in the process of completion. Open Mon-Fri 1-4. Call for information.

Noank Historical Society, 17 Latham Lane, Noank CT 06340, tel (203) 536-3021. Established to preserve the history of Noank. Call for information.

Old Lighthouse Museum, PO Box 103, Stonington CT 06378, tel (203) 535-1440. With prints, paintings and models, this small museum tells the rich history of Stonington as a once important trading and whaling port. Open May-Oct, Tues-Sun 11-4:30. Adults $1, Children 50¢.

US Coast Guard Museum, Waesche Hall, US Coast Guard Academy, Rte. 32, New London CT 06320, tel (203) 444-8511. Located on Academy grounds, the museum displays paintings, models and artifacts that highlight the history of the Coast Guard. Open all year, Mon-Fri 8-4, Sat, Sun and holidays 10-5.

Wethersfield Historical Society, Inc., 150 Main St., Wethersfield CT 06109, tel (203) 529-7656. The Society operates six properties of general interest and a research library at the above address. Open Mon-Fri 1-4, Sat. 12-5.

DELAWARE, Wilmington
Kalmar Nyckel Shipyard and Museum

To bring to life and attract attention to the heritage of "New Sweden"–the first permanent European settlement in the Delaware River Valley.

When complete, the 91-foot, 280-ton replica pinnace *Kalmar Nyckel* will join the current living history shipyard, settler's site, and museum. The shipyard and museum occupy 2.7 acres, with 1,600 square feet of exhibit space in the museum. The research library contains over 2,000 books on Sweden, colonial ships, voyages and settlements.

Exhibits: The ship's construction has created a wealth of craftsmanship in action—attracting shipwrights, wood carvers, shipsmiths, riggers and sail-makers, as well as many willing to learn. Traditional techniques are perpetuated through the museum's apprentice program and are available to the public in semi-annual workshops. Within the museum buildings are exhibits on 17th-century shipbuilding tools, ship plans, flags, navigation, regional Indian and prehistoric artifacts, shipyard archaeology digs and marine artifacts from 1700-1900. The foundation has a few small vessels it maintains and preserves: *Little Key*, an 18-foot ship's boat; *King's Launch*, a 25-foot Swedish naval whale-boat; and a 26-foot Norwegian "Folk Boat."

Schedule: Year round, Monday-Saturday 10am-4pm.
Admission: Adults $2, Seniors and Students $1.

Kalmar Nyckel Foundation
823 E. 7th St., Wilmington DE 19801
(302) 429-0350   Malcolm Mackenzie, Director

DELAWARE

Battle of the Atlantic Memorial, Foot of King Street on Christina River, Wilmington DE; mailing address: 901 Washington St., Wilminton DE 19801, tel (302) 656-0400. The 153-foot US Coast Guard Cutter *Mohawk*, built in 1943, is restored, operational and open to the public with an onboard display on her history and the Battle of the Atlantic. Open Saturdays year round 9-4. Admission: $1.

Overfalls Lightship, c/o Lewes Historical Society, Third Street, Lewes DE 19958, tel (302) 645-6708. Built in 1938 in East Boothbay, Maine. Call for information.

The Navy Museum

To inform, educate, and inspire the public in the traditions, heritage, and scientific contributions of the naval service.

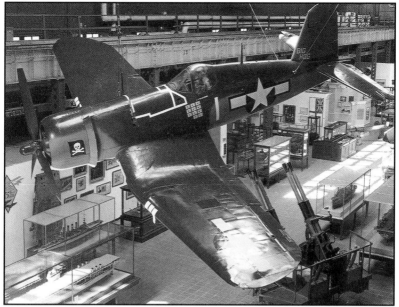

A World War II Corsair overlooking the museum's exhibit hall.

The Navy Museum was established in 1961 by Admiral Arleigh Burke and is housed in part of the former gun factory in the Washington Navy Yard. This 600 foot long building provides 40,000 square feet of exhibit space for more than 3,000 artifacts. The museum is part of the Center for Naval History which includes research, archival, curatorial, photographic and library branches.

Exhibits: Exhibits chronicle the history of the US Navy from the Revolution to the Space Age. There are extensive displays commemorating the Navy's wartime heroes and battles along with its peacetime contributions to exploration, diplomacy, space flight, and navigation. The museum has notable paintings, dioramas, ship models, naval guns, and airplanes; also of special interest are artifacts from famous vessels, including a fighting top from the *Constitution*, items from the *Maine*, and an anchor from the carrier *Enterprise*.

Vessels: USS *Barry* (DD-933), a 418-foot *Forrest Sherman*-class destroyer, a recent addition to the Navy Yard, is now open to the public.

Location: Building 76 of the Washington Navy Yard. Enter through the main gate at 9th and M Streets, SE.

Schedule: Year round (except some holidays), Mon-Fri 9am-4pm (9-5 in the Summer), weekends and holidays 10am-5pm.   **Admission:** Free.

Picnic Area	**The Navy Museum**
Restaurant	Building 76, Washington Navy Yard
Gift Shop	Washington DC 20374
Free Parking	(202) 433-4882
Officer's Club	Dr. Oscar P. Fitzgerald, Director

DISTRICT OF COLUMBIA, Washington
National Museum of American History, Smithsonian Institution

To illuminate, through collections, exhibitions, research, publications and educational programs, the entire history of the United States, including the external influences that have helped to shape the national character.

The American History Museum, part of the Smithsonian complex, has two halls that deal directly and extensively with maritime history–the Hall of American Maritime Enterprise, and the Hall of Armed Forces History.

Exhibits: The Hall of American Maritime Enterprise features American maritime history from the colonial period to the present. Displays cover both broad and specific topics, from whole eras to individuals, bringing scenes alive with models, paintings and artifacts. Part of the Armed Forces History Hall explores our naval heritage, also with a collection of models and artifacts. Of special interest is the Revolutionary gunboat *Philadelphia*, which was raised from Lake Champlain in 1935. The Divisions of Armed Forces History and Transportation offer specialized library and research facilities. The Museum holds lectures, educational programs and changing exhibits year round.

Schedule: Year round, daily except Christmas, 10-5:30.   **Admission:** Free.

National Museum of American History
Smithsonian Institution, Washington DC 20560
(202) 357-2025   Roger Kennedy, Director

DISTRICT OF COLUMBIA

US Marine Corps Museum, Washington Navy Yard, Bldg. 58, Ninth & M Streets SE, Washington DC 20374, tel (202) 433-3840. The history of the Corps is brought to life with 40 display cases and panels exhibiting uniforms, weapons, art, documents and photographs. The exhibit area occupies about 17,600 sq ft. Research facilities include collections of personal papers, art and a library of over 30,000 volumes. Open every day except Christmas and New Years, 10-4, Sundays 12-5. Admission is free.

Museum of Man in the Sea

To preserve the history of diving technology and to be a teaching center for visitors and students alike, in which they learn of man's struggle to live, work, and play underwater.

The Museum was founded in 1982 and opened at its present location in 1987. A 4,000-square foot building houses the permanent collection and one or more special collections. A full-time director and two part-time staff members manage the museum, give tours, and are in the process of organizing and expanding the collection of professional books, magazines and manuals.

Exhibits: The permanent collection of commercial, government, and sport diving equipment includes the original *Sealab I*, Mark I deep dive system, helmets, full diving dress, old air pumps, armored diving suit and many others. Tapes, photographs and charts as well as artifacts are used in the special exhibits "Treasures from the Spanish Galleons" and "Aquanauts to Astronauts."

Schedule: Year round, every day 9am-5pm.   **Admission:** Adults $3.50, Children (6-16) $1.50, Discount of 10% for Seniors and Groups.

Museum of Man in the Sea
17314 Back Beach Road (Hwy 98), Panama City Beach FL 32413
(904) 235-4101   Douglas R. Hough

FLORIDA

HMS Bounty, PO Box 114224, Miami FL 33111. Replica of 18th century Royal Navy vessel famous for the mutiny against Capt. Bligh, built for 1960 movie version of "Mutiny on the Bounty." Open to the public when not on tour. Write for information.

Key West Lighthouse Museum, Harbor Entrance, 989 Whitehead St., Key West FL 33040, tel (305) 294-0012. Restored lighthouse contains exhibits on regional history, including artifacts from local shipwrecks. Open year round, 9:30-5 daily. Adults $3, Children $1.

Key West Maritime Historical Society, 1009 South St., Key West FL 33040, tel (305) 292-7903. Call or write for information.

Museum of Florida History, R.A.Gray Bldg.,Tallahassee FL 32301, tel (904) 488-1484. A museum of general Florida history, it contains exhibits on steamboats and canoes, and it displays artifacts and treasures salvaged from Spanish ships wrecked on the Florida coast.

Naval Aviation Museum, Naval Air Station, Pensacola FL 32509, tel (904) 452-3604. Located on the grounds of the nation's oldest naval air station, the museum depicts the history of naval aviation since its beginnings in Pensacola in 1914. Restored aircraft, ship models and photographs are on display. Open daily 9-5. Admission is free.

FLORIDA

Pensacola Historical Museum, Old Christ Church, 405 S. Adams St., Pensacola FL 32501, tel (904) 432-1559. Chronological exhibits cover regional history from the first Indians to the beginning of the 20th century. Library contains files on shipping and fishing industries. Extensive photographic collections of the port of Pensacola with emphasis on turn-of-the-century sailing ships. Open year round, Mon-Sat 9-4. Admission is free.

The Wrecker's Museum, 322 Duval St., Key West FL 33040, tel (305) 294-9502. The museum building is the 1829 house of a sea-captain/wrecker. Key West's "wreckers" were men who would put out to sea in any weather to save lives, cargoes and vessels from the reefs. Their story is told through guides and exhibits of documents, licenses, rules, and colorful paintings illustrating their daring exploits. The house is furnished with original family antiques, ship models, paintings, and artifacts from local wrecks. Open year round, daily 10-4. Adults $2, Children 50¢

GEORGIA, Columbus
Confederate Naval Museum
To preserve and interpret the history of the Confederate States Navy.

On the Chattahoochee River, about 200 miles up from the Gulf of Mexico, the Confederate Navy Built a shipyard at Columbus—relatively safe from seaborne Union raids. Today the small Confederate Naval Museum there displays remains of the 225-ft ironclad ram CSS *Jackson* and 130-ft gunboat CSS *Chattahoochee*. Both were built in the area and raised from the river in the early 1960s.

CSS Alabama.

Exhibits & Vessels: The Museum portrays the maritime aspect of the Confederacy's struggle to stand up to Northern industrial superiority. The vessels, exhibited in an outdoor pavilion, have sad stories of their own, indicative of the true desperation of the cause—one was burned by Union raiders uncompleted after nearly three years of construction, the other scuttled to prevent her capture. Inside exhibits contain dioramas, ship models, Confederate Navy relics, and a number of artifacts recovered from the two ships. All facets of the CSN's development and operations are covered, with special attention to the Confederacy's specially adapted underdog tactics.

Schedule: Year-round; Tues-Sat 10am-5pm, Sun 2-5pm. **Admission:** Free.

Confederate Naval Museum
PO Box 1022, 101 4th Street, Columbus GA 31902
(404) 327-9798   Robert A. Holcombe, Director

Ships of the Sea Museum

Preserving maritime artifacts and other objects relating to 2,000 years of man's historic quest to rule the sea.

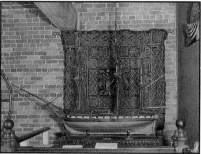

The museum opened in 1966, just across the street from the Savannah River in the heart of the city's historic waterfront district. Its presentation is general, displaying materials that "relate to the mystique of the sea and the ships that sail it." Sixty-five ship models and a ship-in-a-bottle collection represent ships from many ages and all parts of the world. Figureheads, ships' wheels, and other items brought to Savannah by ocean-roaming merchant ships, display many facets of the seafaring world and work to recreate its atmosphere. The museum also has a marine art collection, ship's chandlery, shipwright's shop and small library—all presenting general maritime themes. The building is of historical interest, as a former cotton, lumber, and resin warehouse. An exhibit explores these three exports, which helped make Savannah the major seaport of the South in the 19th century.

Schedule: Year-round, every day 10am-5pm.
Admission (suggested donation): Adults $2, Children 75¢.

Ships of the Sea Museum, 503 East River Street, Savannah GA 31401
(912) 232-1511   David T. Guernsey, Jr., Director

GEORGIA

Coastal Heritage Society, 601 W. Harris St., Savannah GA 31401, tel (912) 232-3945. Small museum inside Old Fort Jackson tells the history of the fort and local coastal region. Call for hours.

Museum of Coastal History, 101 12th St., PO Box 1136, St. Simons Island GA 31522, tel (912) 638-3666. Housed in an 1872 lighthouse keeper's cottage, the museum explores the heritage of the south Georgia coastal region. Presentation includes changing exhibits on topics of local interest. Archives contain photographs, artifacts, manuscripts and maps. Year-round, Mon-Sat 10-5, Sun l:30-5. Adults $1.50, Children $1.

US Navy Supply Corps Museum, US Navy Supply Corps School, Prince Ave. & Oglethorpe St., Athens GA 30606-5000, (404) 354-7343. Exhibits present the growth and development of the Supply Corps and explain its many and varied functions in supplying today's navy. Displays feature ship models, uniforms, navigational equipment, paintings and personal memorabilia. A small archives (photos, official records) and library (yearbooks, manuals, newsletters) are attached to the museum. Year round, Mon-Fri 8:30-5. Admission free.

Hawaii Maritime Center

To preserve the maritime heritage of Hawaii, insure broad-based dissemination of ocean-related information, and support appropriate related cultural, educational, and social programs.

Falls of Clyde and Kalakaua Boathouse, 1988.

Since its founding in 1976, the Maritime Center has acquired the *Falls of Clyde* and built a 27,000-square foot museum facility—the Kalakaua Boat House—on Pier 7 in Honolulu Harbor. This extensive recent development is the initial project in the revitalization of the Honolulu waterfront. The Center has over 1500 books, 10,000 photographs, 1,000 members and a $1,000,000 budget.

Exhibits, Programs & Events: The Kalakaua Boat House contains some 35 major exhibits, telling the entire story of Hawaii's maritime past—from the original discovery by Polynesians on voyaging canoes to the present day. The upper floor deals primarily with Hawaiian history since Western arrival, covering early trade, naval history, the islands' role as a major whaling center, inter-island trade, commercial fishing, and many other aspects. First floor exhibits are primarily engaged in presenting Hawaiian maritime culture— voyaging and migration, traditional fishing, surfing, tattooing, Hawaiian folk medicine, etc. Special displays include a 45-foot Koa and glass double-hulled canoe case, a map of Polynesian migration, and videotapes of island surfing and windsurfing. A Walkman audio tour is included with admission. The Center holds lectures and hosts programs with local groups throughout the year.

Vessels: Moored alongside the boathouse is *Falls of Clyde*, the last remaining four-masted full-rigged ship, and sole surviving sail-driven oil tanker. Her career included service in the sugar trade, the oil trade, and as a passenger vessel between Hawaii and California. Also moored alongside is *Hokule'a*, a full-scale replica of a Polynesian voyaging canoe. She has sailed throughout the Pacific since 1976, using non-instrument navigation methods, and has helped prove the theory of island-settlement-by-canoe. She remains at the Center to rekindle and preserve ancient Polynesian skills and traditions.

Schedule: Year round except Christmas, every day 9am-8pm.
Admission: Adults $6, Children (6-17) $3, Children under 6 free.

Membership	**Hawaii Maritime Center**
Gift Shop	Pier 7, Honolulu HI 96813
Restaurant	(808) 523-6151
Free Parking	Evarts C. Fox, Jr., PhD, Director

USS Arizona Memorial

To preserve the history of USS Arizona *and the causes and effects of America's entry into WWII based on the Japanese attack at Pearl Harbor; and to memorialize the casualties of that attack.*

Administered by the National Park Service, the USS Arizona Memorial and its shoreside museum form part of a sprawling visitor center overlooking Pearl Harbor and historic Battleship Row. Boat tours every 15-20 minutes take visitors to the memorial, which spans the submerged wreck. The memorial opened in 1962, and the museum in 1980. The complex receives over 1.5 million visitors a year.

Exhibits: USS *Arizona*'s anchor and bell, a 50-foot mural of the ship, and a few WWII ship models are displayed in the museum. Memorabilia and battle souvenirs are used in exhibits designed to tell the story of Hawaii and the Battlship Navy prior to WWII, during the attack, and in early Pacific-theater battles. A film and talks by Park Service Rangers and Pearl Harbor veterans complement a tour of the museum and memorial.

Schedule: Year round, closed some holidays; Visitor Center: 7:30am-5:00pm. Boat tour: 8:00am-3:00pm. **Admission:** Free.

USS Arizona Memorial
1 Arizona Memorial Pl., Honolulu HI 96818
(808) 422-2771   Donald E. Magee, Superintendent

HAWAII

Bernice P. Bishop Museum, PO Box 19000-A, 1525 Bernice St., Honolulu HI 96817, tel (808) 847-3511. Displays explore the natural and cultural history of Hawaii and the Pacific, with the islands' maritime history well represented in both the museum and its library. Museum open year round, daily 9-5. Library open Tues-Fri 10-3.

Carthaginian II, 890 Alva St., Wailuku HI 96793, tel (808) 661-8527. This fully restored brig of 1901 is berthed at the wharf at the end of Dickinson Street in historic Lahaina harbor. A museum has a video presentation and preserved whaling boat. Open daily 9-4.

Pacific Submarine Museum, 11 Arizona Memorial Drive, Honolulu HI 96818, tel (808) 423-1341. The museum and submarine USS *Bowfin* are part of a memorial park dedicated to the US submariners lost during World War II. Chronological exhibits cover pre-20th century submarines through post-WWII and into the future. Displays include photos, art, models, books, flags and equipment from subs. Open year round, daily 8-5. Adults $6, Children $1.

IDAHO

SS *Jean*, c/o Friends of the Jean, 3112 Seventh St., Lewiston ID 83501, tel (208) 743-2344. Berthed on the Snake River along Hell's Gate State Park, this 169-ft, sternwheel tug of 1938 has undergone extensive restoration since her move from Portland harbor to Lewiston. Once a site of many community events, she is closed and restoration has been halted. Future plans are unclear.

21

ILLINOIS, Chicago
Chicago Maritime Museum

Featuring the travel and commerce of the Great Lakes, Chicago as port city and anchor for western expansion, and the inland canals and waterways of the middle west.

The museum is run by the Chicago Maritime Society. It is located at North Pier Chicago, a multi-purpose festival marketplace which was renovated from a freight terminal and is a valuable remnant of Chicago's historic river port.

Exhibits & Vessels: The main exhibit, "Port to Port," illustrates 300 years of Great Lakes trade and commerce. Most exhibits are kept on a relatively temporary basis and some are reports of the Society's activities. Among the current ones are: Christmas Tree Ships, People of Chicago's Port, Steamboating in Style, The Eastland Disaster, Chicago's Port in 1983, and Underwater Archaeology. Also on display are over 70 small watercraft, showing the wide range of boats used in the mid-west during the past century. As part of the Maritime Society, the museum devotes much energy to promoting educational programs and research and to sponsoring community activities, which include lectures, workshops, outings, forums, and the annual Chicago Maritime Festival.

Schedule: Year round, Tuesday-Sunday Noon-5pm. **Admission:** Free.

Chicago Maritime Museum/Maritime Society
455 East Illinois St., Chicago IL 60611
(312) 836-4343   Barton Updike, Acting Director

ILLINOIS, Lockport
Illinois and Michigan Canal Museum

To present the complete story of the canal, including its planning, development, construction, operation, and impact on the lifestyles and growth of the region.

The museum is housed in the original office and residential building of the I&M Canal Commission, built in 1837 in the town of Lockport. The town is considered to be the best-preserved canal town in the nation and is a National Register Historic District.

Exhibits: Exhibits are separated into 14 areas, exploring the industry, agriculture and social life that thrived around the canal, along with an explanation of the necessity of waterway travel for the early settlers. Part of the building is maintained completely in its original residential setting, with 19th and early 20th century furnishings. There is also a scale replica of *City of Pekin*, one of the largest boats to travel the canal. In June the Museum holds an open house during the town's Old Canal Days festival.

Schedule: Year round, every day 1pm-4:30pm.   **Admission:** Free.

Illinois and Michigan Canal Museum
803 South State St., Lockport IL 60441
(815) 538-5080   Rose V. Bucciferro, Director

Museum of Science and Industry

The Museum demonstrates scientific principles, technological advances and industrial applications—stressing visitor participation and using the most modern exhibit technology available.

Founded in 1955, the museum is located along Lake Michigan on Chicago's south side. It is one of the world's largest museums of science and technology, with over 2,000 exhibit units in 75 halls. The maritime aspect of technological history is presented in two exhibit halls and claims the museum's proudest possession, a captured WWII German U-boat.

Exhibits & Vessels: The 252-foot, 1,144-ton submarine U-505 was brought to Chicago in 1954 and is currently on display outside adjacent to the Sea Power hall. A new self-guided tour features narration by U-boat crew members and US veterans involved in her dramatic capture. Inside, displays range from a reproduction of USS *Constitution*'s gundeck to modern naval missile systems. "Ships through the Ages" hall presents an overview of the entire history of marine transportation, displaying many shipmodels and a full-size reproduction of a merchant ship's wooden mizzenmast.

Schedule: Year round, every day except Christmas; Summer, weekends & holidays 9:30am-5:30pm; Rest of the year 9:30am-4pm. **Admission:** Museum is free. Submarine $2.50.

Museum of Science and Industry, 57th Street & Lake Shore Drive
Chicago IL 60637   (312) 684-1414

ILLINOIS

Viking Ship Restoration Committee, Inc., 518 Davis St., Evanston IL 60201, tel (708) 492-1829. The committee plans to restore the 1893 replica longship which was sailed from Norway to Newfoundland by Capt. Magnus Andersen. Now in Victory Park, plans are to move the vessel to Chicago's Museum of Science and Industry (see above).

INDIANA

Howard Steamboat Museum, c/o Clark County Historical Society, PO Box 606, 1100 Market St., Jeffersonville IN 47130, tel (812) 283-3728. The museum commemorates the Howard Shipyard (in operation from 1834 to 1941), and includes several models, shipyard tools, photographs, documents and steamboat memorabilia. Open year round, Tues-Sun.

Old Lighthouse Museum, Heisman Harbor Road, Washington Park, PO Box 512, Michigan City, IN 46360, tel (219) 872-6133. The lighthouse, restored by the Michigan City Historical Society, houses a museum on the history of Michigan City, along with changing displays. Small research library available by appointment. Open year round, Tues-Sun 1-4. Adults $2, Children 50¢.

Whitewater Canal State Historic Site, c/o Indiana State Museum, 202 North Alabama St., Indianapolis IN 46264, tel (317) 647-6512. A park surrounds a 14-mile stretch of the canal originally dug to connect the Ohio River and Lake Erie. Canalboat rides are offered, and a small museum is housed in a gristmill which is part of the restored Metamora Canal Village.

IOWA, Keokuk
Keokuk River Museum

To display and preserve the history and artifacts of riverboats—especially those of the upper Mississippi River.

The museum is located in Victory Park on the banks of the Mississippi. It is contained entirely within the *Geo. M. Verity*, a 578-ton, 162-foot steam sternwheel towboat from the upper Mississippi River barge service. She is one of only three remaining out of a class that once numbered almost 1,500.

Exhibits: The *Geo. M. Verity*, retired since 1960, is in good condition and is completely accessible to the public. Visitors can examine the original boiler, all machinery, the crew's quarters, and a pilot house. In the onboard exhibits are photos of steamboats and modern diesel riverboats, steam whistles, pilot wheels, caulking tools, documents, SID reflectors, and a library of river books and waterways journals.

Schedule: April 1 to October 31, every day 9am-4pm.

Admission: Adults $1.50, Children (6-14) 75¢, Children under 6 free.

Keokuk River Museum
Victory Park on the river front, PO Box 400, Keokuk IA 52632
(319) 524-4765   Robert L. Miller, Director

IOWA, Dubuque
Woodward Riverboat Museum

To explore, collect, preserve, and interpret, for present and future generations, the history of Dubuque County and the Upper Mississippi River, and—through the National Rivers Hall of Fame—the history of the inland waters.

The Dubuque County Historical Society presides over The Port of Dubuque River Museums, which consists of the Woodward Riverboat Museum, the sidewheeler *William M. Black*, the National Rivers Hall of Fame and the Mathias Ham House. The Society has 13,000 square feet of exhibit space in buildings along the river in Ice Harbor.

Exhibits & Vessels: The museum's main maritime exhibits cover the history of the Upper River and the surrounding valley civilization. These include studies of typical riverboats, the evolution of river craft, early explorers, river fishing, and the resources of the land which fed the river's bustling activity. Berthed alongside the museum, the 277-ft sidewheeler *William M. Black* is completely accessible to the public. A number of small craft are also on display.

Schedule: May-Oct, daily 10am-6:30pm; Nov-April, 10am-4pm.
William M. Black closed in Winter.   **Admission:** Adults $4, Children $1.

Port of Dubuque River Museums
2nd Street, Ice Harbor, PO Box 305, Dubuque IA 52001
(319) 557-9545   Jerome A. Enzler, Director

IOWA

Buffalo Bill Museum of Le Claire, Inc., 200 N. River Drive, Le Claire IA 52753, tel (319) 289-5580. The main exhibit, SS *Lone Star*, is one of the few survivng wooden-hulled river boats, a former wood-burning sidewheeler converted to coal-burning sternwheeler and retired in 1968. Museum exhibits explore the history of the upper Mississippi River with boat models, photographs, shipboard tools and artifacts. Other exhibits on local history. Open summer daily, 9-4:30; rest of year, weekends only 9-4:30. Adults $1, Children 50¢.

Putnam Museum, 1717 West 12th St., Davenport IA 52804, tel (319) 324-1933. Of maritime interest is the regional history exhibit "River, Prairie and People." Maritime artifacts are on display in a gallery overlooking the river. A computer program provides access to many other photographs and artifacts. Open year round, Tues-Sat 9-5, Sun 1-5. Adults $2, Children and Seniors $1.

***City of Clinton* Showboat**, 1401 Eleventh Ave. North, Clinton IA 52732, tel (319) 243-1260. The former sternwheel steam tug of 1935 now houses a small theater and exhibit of steamboat artifacts and photographs. Portions of the vessel are open to the public. Out of water year round. Call for information.

KENTUCKY

Steamer *Belle of Louisville*, 4th Ave. & River Road, Louisville KY 40202, tel (502) 625-2355. Built in 1914 as a ferry and day packet, the 170-ft *Belle* makes daily cruises 2-4pm. Steamboat memorabilia are on the main deck; the engine room is open to visitors Call for rates and additional schedule information.

New Orleans, LOUISIANA
Louisiana State Museum

To collect, preserve and present Louisiana's unique cultural heritage through artifacts, works of art and documents.

Established in 1911, the Museum consists of ten landmark properties in three Louisiana cities, with significant collections of furniture, maps and documents, Civil War materials, and Native American artifacts relating to general Louisiana history. Two of its buildings, the Presbytere and Old US Mint in New Orleans feature exhibitions of Louisiana and New Orleans history, exploring a number of maritime themes, including New Orleans' significant role as a riverine and deepwater port.

The collection's most prominent maritime possession is a Civil War submarine once believed to be the confederate sub *Pioneer* (its true identity is now a subject of debate) on display just outside the Presbytere. Paintings and ship models in both buildings depict ocean-going and river vessels. The rest of the maritime collection focuses primarily on the Mississippi River and its powerful influence on history and culture in the region.

Schedule: Year round,Wed-Sun 10am-5pm. **Admission:** Adults $3, Seniors & Teens $1.50, Children under 12 free.

Louisiana State Museum, Box 2448, New Orleans LA 70176-2448
(504) 568-6968   James F. Sefcik, Director

LOUISIANA, Baton Rouge
Louisiana Naval War Memorial & Nautical Center

To preserve Louisiana's naval and maritime history through the restoration of USS Kidd and the acquisition, protection, and exhibition of materials for the use and enjoyment of the public.

Destroyer USS *Kidd* is berthed along the Mississippi River, adjacent to the Nautical Center and a memorial to the 7,000 Louisianians killed in foreign wars.

USS *Kidd* (DD-661) is a *Fletcher*-class destroyer, commissioned in 1943. She served with valor in the Pacific theater, was recalled for Korean service in 1951 and decommissioned in 1964. Today, she is kept in her 1945 configuration and houses the center's collection of WWII uniforms, artifacts, tools, weaponry, charts and documents which illustrate life aboard US Navy destroyers in WWII. The Nautical Center also has displays from the collection of the former Louisiana Maritime Museum, which contains ship models, prints, paintings and books. The Center holds two annual memorial services and hosts overnight camping programs for youth groups.

Schedule: Year round, seven days a week 9am-5pm.
Admission: Adults $3.50, Seniors $2.50, Children $2.

Louisiana Naval War Memorial & Nautical Center
305 S. River Road, Baton Rouge LA 70802
(504) 342-1942   Timothy Rizzuto, Acting Director

LOUISIANA

Delta Queen Steamboat Company, Home Port Office, #30 Robin Street Wharf, New Orleans LA 70130, tel (504) 586-0631. The last remaining river steamboat line offering overnight passages on two vessels: The *Delta Queen* of 1926 and the *Mississippi Queen* of 1976. Both vessels make 3- to 14-night cruises on the Mississippi, Ohio, Cumberland and Tennessee rivers. There are onboard exhibits of photographs and artifacts from the golden age of steam. Call for schedule of cruises and rate information.

Maine Maritime Museum

To serve as the major repository for the preservation of Maine's maritime artifacts and archives, with collections and exhibitions interpreting the role of Maine ships and sailors in national and international maritime affairs since 1607.

In 1989, with the completion of the 30,000 sq ft Maritime History building, the museum was relocated and united on a single 10-acre site along the Kennebec River. There, it encompasses ten buildings, including five historic shipyard structures. In 1989 the museum had 80,000 visitors, 21 full-time staff, 200 volunteers, 3,000 members and a $900,000 budget.

Exhibits: Virtually every aspect of Maine's rich maritime heritage is represented in the museum's exhibitions in the Maritime History Building—from local shipbuilders and world-voyagers to the daily challenges of earning a living on the rugged Maine coast. Collections also cover a wide range of general maritime themes—with more than 200 paintings and ship portraits, 250 half-hull and fully rigged ship models, along with fishing and shipbuilding gear, nautical instruments, scrimshaw, porcelain, silver and seafarers' souvenirs from around the world.

Shipyard Buildings & Vessels: Five buildings of the Percy and Small Shipyard have been restored to their turn-of-the-century condition. Kept in use by the museum's Apprenticeshop, they serve as a living reminder and active participant in the vivid story of Maine shipbuilding. Exhibits in the working saw mill, paint and treenail shop, caulking shed and mold loft describe and interpret the process by which the yard produced its large commercial schooners in the late 19th/early 20th century. Another building contains the exhibit "Lobstering and the Maine Coast," featuring the history of lobstering, including canning, live shipment, traps, and boats. A collection of more than 100 small craft, ranging from the pinky-schooner *Maine* to small dinghies and gunning floats are kept in the Smallcraft/Apprenticeshop Building and berthed at the museum's pier. Also frequently berthed there in the summer is the *Sherman Zwicker*, a 142-foot Grand Banks fishing schooner owned by the Grand Banks Schooner Museum

Programs & Events: The Apprenticeshop runs a 12-month study course in traditional boatbuilding skills. The Museum offers a wide range of educational programs, maritime history symposiums, lectures, workshops, and school programs. Daily Events: Operation of boatyard facilities, river sailing by apprentices on Kennebec, operation of antique engines, and cruises on the river. Special Events: Boatbuilding and crafts demonstrations, launchings, guided tours of buildings, music festivals, concerts, visiting vessels, and regattas.

Location: Mid-coast Maine, 10 miles up the Kennebec River.

Schedule: Year round, every day 9:30am-5:00pm.

Admission: Adults $5, Children $2.50, Seniors and group discounts.

Maine Maritime Museum
243 Washington Street, Bath ME 04530
(207) 443-1316   Jean M. Weber, Director

MAINE, Searsport
Penobscot Marine Museum

To collect and preserve materials, marine paintings and artifacts relating to the maritime activity of Maine and the nation; to publish materials and support a comprehensive educational program about our seafaring heritage.

Founded in 1936, the museum consists of seven historic buildings on the northwest shore of Penobscot Bay on the Maine Coast. The museum has eight full-time and 22 part-time employees, with a $380,000 annual budget and 1,000 members. An art gallery and 6,000-volume research library, containing an extensive geneological collection, are open year round.

Exhibits, Programs & Events: The museum originated and grew around collections of artwork, artifacts, and documents from the homes of local master mariners. Currently in the collection are 50 ship models of local area vessels, 25 figureheads, a scrimshaw collection, and over 450 paintings—including works by Thomas and James Buttersworth, Antonio Jacobsen, and Fredric Cozzens. The museum's exhibits tell the story of Penobscot Bay and the entire Maine coast, giving special attention to the lives and achievements of local seafarers. On display are numerous local artifacts, shipbuilding tools, and navigational instruments. Large dioramas of 19th century Searsport harbor and shipyards and several examples of period furniture are especially interesting. A year-round schedule of events includes lectures and concerts, museums-in-schools programs, and summer programs in education.

Vessels: 24 Penobscot Bay small craft are on display, along with a few 40-foot workboats and outfits of the smelting fishery.

Location: Corner of Route 1 and Church Street in Searsport, on Penobscot Bay, about 20 miles south of Bangor and halfway along the Maine coast.

Schedule: May 15 through October 15, Monday-Saturday 9:30am-5:00pm, Sunday 1:00pm-5:00pm.

Admission: Adults $4, Seniors $3.50, Children (7-15) $1.50.

Membership
Gift Shop
Picnic Area
Free Parking

Penobscot Marine Museum
Church Street
Searsport ME 04974
(207) 548-2529
Renny A. Stackpole, Director

Kittery Historical and Naval Museum

To collect, preserve and display artifacts of significance to the maritime and cultural heritage of Kittery and its region.

Inspired by the Bicentennial, this museum was established in 1976 to interpret the history of Maine's oldest town. Kittery was settled by seafarers and merchant entrepreneurs ca 1623, and the town was incorporated in 1647. Collections include artifacts, books, photographs and other documents.

Exhibits: Featured are objects from three centuries of Kittery history, its maritime and shipbuilding tradition as well as colonial crafts and Americana. Exhibits explore archaeological evidence of early settlements; mercantile success of local families, notably that of William Pepperrell and his honored son, Sir William Pepperrell; and the history of the Portsmouth Naval Shipyard, which was established in Kittery in 1806. On display are numerous ship models, navigational gear, household artifacts, toys and more.

Schedule: May-Oct, Mon-Fri 10am-4pm; November-April by appointment.
Admission: Adults $2, Children $1.

Kittery Historical and Naval Museum
PO Box 453, Rogers Rd., Kittery ME 03904
(207) 439-3080   Patricia Q. Wall, Director

Shore Village Museum

Preserving lighthouses, the history and artifacts from lighthouses, and the maritime history of the Maine coast.

Founded in 1978, the Museum has the largest collection of lighthouse artifacts on display in America—many of these rescued from destruction with the advent of automated lights and beacons. The museum building was donated by the Daughters of Union Veterans, and a few exhibits are kept on Rockland's Fourth Maine Regiment of the Union Army.
Exhibits: The museum's central theme is maritime safety, emphasizing navigational aids of the Maine coast. Displayed in "Coast Guard Rooms," exhibits include lights, lenses, lighthouse machinery, and life saving gear from rescue boats and stations. One of the most outstanding items is a 10-ft tall second-order Fresnel lens, built in 1855 for Petit Manan, the largest light tower on the Maine coast. Other maritime exhibits include ship models, fishing gear, scrimshaw, nautical instruments, photos, paintings and watercolor prints of lighthouses and light ships, records of merchant ships and Civil War naval vessels.

Schedule: June 1-Oct 15, every day 10am-4pm. **Admission:** Free.

Shore Village Museum
104 Limerock Street, Rockland ME 04841
(207) 594-0311   Robert N. Davis, Curator

MAINE, South Portland
Spring Point Museum

To collect, preserve, display, and interpret memorabilia, artifacts, records, and other information of historical significance to Portland Harbor, Casco Bay and bordering towns.

Founded in 1986, the Museum is a cooperative effort of the South Portland/Cape Elizabeth Historical Society, the South Portland Shipyard Historical Society, and the Clipper Ship *Snow Squall* Project. The museum is housed in Fort Preble, a former coastal defense installation, located on the campus of Southern Maine Technical College on the shore of Casco Bay.

Exhibits: Artifacts of the three component organizations comprise a core exhibit on regional history. This contains photo displays, ship models, shipbuilding tools and occasional special exhibits. A very significant artifact on display is a 35-foot portion of the bow of the clipper ship *Snow Squall*—the last remaining piece of an American-built extreme clipper. Built in South Portland in 1851, *Snow Squall* was beached in the Falklands in 1864, where she remained until her bow was returned to Maine in 1987. Guided tours are given of the conservation laboratory where timbers and artifacts from the ship are preserved.

Schedule: June-October, Wed-Sun 1pm-4pm; off-season by appointment.

Admission: Adults $2, Children under 12 and members free.

Spring Point Museum, SMTC, Fort Road, South Portland ME 04106
(207) 799-6337   William A. Bayreuther, Director

MAINE

Allie Ryan Collection of the Maine State Museum, c/o Maine Maritime Academy, Castine ME 04420, tel (207) 326-4331. On display is the extensive collection of the late Allie Ryan, consisting mainly of prints, photos, models and hundreds of paintings of coastal shipping from Penobscot Bay. Call for hours.

Border Historical Society, 1 Capen Ave., Eastport ME 04631, tel (207) 853-2328. Established to preserve information and artifacts relevant to the history of the US and Canadian shores of Passamaquoddy Bay. Call for information.

Deer Isle-Stonington Historical Society, Stonington ME 04681, tel (207) 637-5012. Established to collect and preserve historic records and artifacts pertaining to Deer Isle, Stonington and adjoining communities. Call for hours.

Friendship Museum, Friendship Sloop Society, Friendship ME 04547, tel (207) 832-4984. A small volunteer-staffed museum housed in a one-room former schoolhouse, the Friendship Museum displays tools, photographs, models and records celebrating the long-standing tradition of the builders, owners and sailors of Friendship sloops. Originally built as sturdy all-weather fishing vessels, Friendship sloops have been appreciated by yachtsmen for their deepwater cruising and racing capabilities. Call for schedule.

Grand Banks Schooner Museum, PO Box 123, Boothbay ME 04537, tel (207) 633-4727. The Museum maintains the *Sherman Zwicker*, a 142-ft auxiliary fishing schooner of 1942. In summer, the vessel is on display at the Maine Maritime Museum and undergoes restoration during the winter. Call for information.

Isleford Historical Museum, c/o Acadia National Park, Bar Harbor ME 04609, tel (207) 288-3338. This small museum, located on Cranberry Island, preserves and displays documents, artifacts, ship models, logs, paintings and lobstering gear. Call for schedule.

Lightship Nantucket, Inc., Suite M, 465 Congress St., Portland ME 04101, tel (207) 775-1181. Lightship #112 is a floating museum, based in Portland, that travels frequently along the eastern seaboard making appearances in other ports. Visitors may tour most of the ship, often with a guide. Exhibits explain the way of life aboard a lightship. Call for current schedule and rates.

Machiasport Historical Society Museum, Gates House, Rte. 92, Machiasport ME 04055, tel (207) 255-8641. Ship models and paintings recount the famous capture of the British warship HMS *Margaretta*, led by Jeremiah O'Brien (the Liberty ship in San Francisco keeps his name alive today). Other exhibits explore the history of Machias Bay, its lumber trade and coasting schooners. Call for information.

Moosehead Marine Museum, PO Box 1151, Greenville ME 04441, tel (207) 695-2716. Located on Moosehead Lake, the museum preserves and operates the 1914 steamer *Katahdin*. An extensive collection of early photographs is displayed aboard and in the small shoreside museum, which also houses memorabilia and historical records of the region. Open summer to early autumn, every day 9-5. Museum admission is free. Cruises on *Katahdin*: Adults $12, Seniors $10, Children $6. Call for schedule and charter information.

Old York Historical Society, PO Box 312, York ME 03909, tel (207) 363-4974. The Society has five museum buildings in York and a research library covering local history, archaeology, architecture and social history. The John Hancock warehouse is currently maintained in its 18th century condition as a customs house and contains a display on maritime occupations. The Society also houses the replica gundalow *Fannie M.* during winter months. Open mid-June to Sept, Tues-Sat 10-4. Adults $2 per building, Children $1 per building.

Peary-MacMillan Arctic Museum, Hubbard Hall, Bowdoin College, Brunswick ME 04011, tel (207) 725-3416. Three galleries celebrate the Arctic expeditions of two Bowdoin Alumni, Robert E. Peary and Donald B. MacMillan. Exhibits include models of their ships, native artifacts and a full-size kayak. Open year round, Tues-Sat 10-5, Sun 2-5. Admission is free.

Willowbrook at Newfield, PO Box 80, Newfield ME 04056, tel (207) 793-2784. This 10-acre 19th century restored village presents many aspects of rural New England life. A marine room displays navigational tools, shipbuilders' tools, uniforms, ship models, paintings, maps and other memorabilia. Several marine engines and about five restored small craft are also on display. Open May15-Sept 30, every day 10-5. Adults $5.50, Students $3.

Calvert Marine Museum

Dedicated to the interaction between culture and the marine environment of the Chesapeake Bay and the Patuxent River estuary. The museum's purpose is to interpret this region through three related themes: paleontology, estuarine biology and maritime history.

Drum Point Lighthouse with boat basin and small craft.

Founded in 1970, the Museum was moved to its current home in 1975. Its nine-acre site includes a 29,000-square foot exhibit building, three administrative buildings, a small craft building, the Drum Point Lighthouse, and a boat basin. The museum also has a 3,000-volume library, an archive, and over 15,000 photographs and slides.

Exhibits: At present, the Museum's maritime history exhibits are the only fully developed aspect of its three-part presentation. These focus primarily on the Solomons area history, with special attention to the crab, oyster and fish industries and trade. They also tell the general history of the area, the War of 1812, regional boatbuilding, marine art, and the variety of local vessels. The collection contains models, artifacts, archival documents, drawings and paintings. Future permanent exhibits will depict marine life and tell the pre-history of the region.

Vessels: The Museum's regional boat collection is displayed in the small craft building. This includes the clamboat *John A. Ryder*, Hooper Island draketail *Penguin*, and several yawl boats, skiffs, punts, and canoes. The oyster buyboat *Wm. B. Tennison* and skipjack *Marie Theresa* are floating exhibits at the waterfront. The three-log canoe *Carla Sue* and a 1956 Cruise Along powerboat are on display in the exhibition building.

Location: State Rte 2 on the Patuxent River, about 60 miles south of Annapolis.
Schedule: May-Sept, daily 10am-5pm; Oct-April, Mon-Fri 10am-4:30pm, Sat-Sun 12-4:30pm.
Admission: General admission $3, harbor cruise on *Wm. B. Tennison* $3.50.

Membership	**Calvert Marine Museum**
Gift Shop	PO Box 97
Refreshments	Solomons MD 20688
Picnic Area	(301) 326-2042
Free Parking	Paula Johnson, Acting Director

Chesapeake Bay Maritime Museum

Dedicated to furthering interest, understanding and appreciation of the culture and maritime heritage of the Chesapeake Bay and its tributaries through ongoing educational activities including collection, documentation, exhibition, research and publication.

The Museum occupies 17 acres on Navy Point in the Miles river, with 48,000 square feet of building space. Founded in 1965, it currently has an annual budget of $965,000, 25 full-time staff members, and a 4,000-volume library.

Exhibits, Programs, & Events: The history of the entire Chesapeake Bay region is presented in exhibits housed in four main buildings: the Chesapeake Bay Building, which contains models, marine art and exhibits; the Small Boat Shed; the Hooper Strait Lighthouse; the Waterfowling Building, which contains decoys, guns and mounted birds. Also on the grounds are the marine railway, boat shop and aquarium. A mechanical propulsion exhibit, currently under construction, will trace the history of steam and gas powered transportation on the Bay. The Howard I. Chapelle Library is open to researchers by appointment. The museum conducts numerous programs throughout the year, from seminars to safe boating courses, and runs many activities including Springfest, Museum Day, and Small Craft Festival.

Vessels: More than 80 Chesapeake Bay small craft are on display in the boat basin and exhibit galleries. Of special interest are the bugeye *Edna E. Lockwood*, skipjack *Rosie Parks*, crab dredger *Old Point*, and a Hooper Island draketail launch *Martha*.

Location: Navy Point, on the eastern shore of Maryland on the Miles River.

Schedule: Summer, daily 10am-5pm; Nov-Dec, daily 10am-4pm, Winter, open only weekends & holidays 10am-4pm; March-April, daily 10am-4pm.

Admission: Adults $5, Seniors $4.50, Children $2.50.

	Chesapeake Bay Maritime Museum
Membership	Navy Point
Gift Shop	PO Box 636
Refreshments	St. Michaels MD 21663
Picnic Area	(301) 745-2916
Free Parking	John R. Valiant, Director

MARYLAND, Baltimore
Baltimore Maritime Museum

To educate the public in the history of the sea and the way of a ship, and to maintain vessels which contribute to this endeavor.

The Museum has no building, but exists in its three vessels moored at Pier III in Baltimore's inner harbor. Founded in 1982, the museum now operates with 15 employees and about 50 volunteers.

Exhibits: The three vessels are preserved in their original operating condition and are completely accessible to the public. The vessels also have exhibits of ship models, artifacts, paintings and other displays which augment the educational experience not only regarding the ship, but life at sea in general. The lightship *Chesapeake* is the center of the museum and houses the Chesapeake Bay Foundation, which provides a live-aboard sea-going environment for school groups. The submarine USS *Torsk*, which served at the end of WWII, is completely open to the public, and the USCGC *Taney* is currently undergoing restoration.

Schedule: Year round, every day 9:30am-4:30pm. **Admission:** Adults $3, Children (5-12) $1.50, Seniors $2.50, Active military free.

Baltimore Maritime Museum
Pier III - Pratt Street, Baltimore MD 21202
(301) 396-3453   Henry A. Lingenfelder, Director

MARYLAND, Sharpsburg
C & O Canal National Historical Park

Started as a dream of passage to western wealth, operated as a conduit of eastern coal, suffering extensive and finally fatal flooding, and saved from conversion to a highway, the Chesapeake and Ohio Canal endures as a National Historical Park—a pathway into history, nature and recreation.

Beside the Potomac River, the C & O Canal stretches 184.5 miles from the mouth of Rock Creek in Georgetown to Cumberland, Maryland, rising 605 feet over 74 locks. The entire canal, its locks and tow path, along with a few significant historic structures are preserved as a park accessible to hikers, cyclists, campers, canoers and boaters. Visitor centers at Georgetown and Great Falls offer guided tours of the canal in a replica mule-drawn canalboat. At Great Falls, there are a 19th century tavern and a small museum with exhibits on the canal's construction, operation, and troubled history. Also of interest is a collection of restored buildings at Four Locks Ranger Station (about halfway up the canal) and the 3,188-foot long Paw Paw Tunnel that cuts through a mountain about twenty miles east of the canal's terminus in Cumberland. These and many other sites and facilities located along the canal can be contacted through the Park's headquarters listed below.

C & O Canal National Historical Park
Box 4, Sharpsburg MD 21782   (301) 739-4200
Gordon V. Gay, Chief of Interpretation & Visitor Services

Radcliffe Maritime Museum

To tell the story of Maryland's maritime past—collecting, preserving, and exhibiting artifacts that invite the public to discover that rich history.

The Museum is part of the Maryland Historical Society's headquarters in downtown Baltimore. At the same location are the Darnell Children's Gallery, Symington Library, and Enoch Pratt House.

Exhibits: A wide array of artifacts, paintings, ship models and visual aids are incorporated into several exhibits. The focus is on Baltimore and the upper Chesapeake region, portraying a broad scope of maritime activities: the hardships of the early settlers on the *Ark* and the *Dove*, the era of tobacco trade, early development of Baltimore's inner harbor, regional boatbuilding, the Baltimore clippers, Chesapeake Bay steamboats, and the modern container port. Reconstructions of a 19th century boatbuilding shed, sail loft, ship chandlery, pilot house, and a 1/3 scale model of a Baltimore clipper are incorporated into the exhibits.

Schedule: Year round, Tues-Fri 11am-4:30pm, Saturday 9am-4:30pm, Sunday (October-April only) 1pm-5pm. **Admission:** Adults $2.50, Children 75¢, Seniors $1. Special rates for families and tour groups.

Radcliffe Maritime Museum, 201 W. Monument St., Baltimore MD 21201
(301) 685-3750   Dr. Mary Ellen Hayward, Director

US Naval Academy Museum

To collect, preserve, and utilize objects and works of art which relate the history and traditions of the US Navy, and the role of the Navy, in war and peace, in defending the ideals of the nation.

The museum occupies 9,000 square feet of exhibit space in Preble Hall on the grounds of the Academy. It has a 2,500-volume library and an area for reserve study collections.

Exhibits: There is a variety of objects from the Navy's past on display, including flags, uniforms, weapons, manuscripts, photographs, ship's instruments, medals, and rare books. The museum has a collection of ship models and marine paintings along

with many special artifacts from well-known events in naval history. The four main collections on display are the Henry Huddleston Rogers ship models, Beverley R. Robinson naval prints, Malcolm Storer naval medals, and U.S. Navy trophy flags. There is also space for special annual exhibitions which are designed to complement the permanent displays.

Schedule: Year round, Mon-Sat 9am-5pm, Sun 11am-5pm. **Admission:** Free.
US Naval Academy Museum, Annapolis MD 21402-5034
(301) 267-2108   Kenneth J. Hagan, Director

MARYLAND

Baltimore Museum of Industry, 1415 Key Highway, Baltimore MD 21230, tel (301) 727-4808. Exhibits explore the industrial, maritime and labor aspects of Baltimore's history. The 1906 steam tug *Baltimore* is under restoration, eventually to return to her pre-WWI condition and to operate a passenger service on the inner harbor. Open year round, Thurs-Sun 12-5; Memorial Day to Labor Day, Tues-Sun 12-5; every Sat 10-5. Adults $2, Students & Seniors $1.

Brown's Wharf Maritime Museum, Rukert Terminals, 2021 South Clinton, Baltimore MD 21224, tel (301) 276-1013. Museum on an old wharf in Baltimore's inner harbor owned by the Rukert Terminals Corp., contains exhibits on the history and development of cargo handling and transportation in Baltimore. Open on special occasions and by appointment. Call for information.

Chesapeake & Delaware Canal Museum, Second St. and Bethel Rd., South Chesapeake City MD 21915, tel (301) 885-5621. In the museum building overlooking the canal, several models and dioramas portray the canal's long history of over 150 years. Maps, artifacts and machinery from the old locks are also on display. Call for information.

Havre de Grace Maritime Museum, 200 Level Rd., Havre de Grace MD 21078, tel (301) 939-1546. A new museum about to begin construction on a new facility. When complete, it will feature the maritime activity of the northern Chesapeake Bay area. The skipjack *Mary W. Sommers* is scheduled for restoration. Call for information.

Historic St. Mary's City, Box 39, Rosecroft Rd., St. Mary's City MD 20686, tel (301) 862-0990. An 840-acre outdoor museum of history, archaeology and natural history located on the site of Maryland's first European settlement and capital. The 76-ft, 50-ton replica pinnace *Maryland Dove*, built to approximate the original *Dove*, one of two ships involved in the city's founding in 1634, is berthed at a pier on the site, along with a replica jolly boat and colonial log canoe. Open spring and autumn weekends only 10-5; summer, Wed-Sun 10-5. Adults $4, Seniors $2, Children $1.50.

Longship Company, Ltd., Oakley Farm, Avenue MD 10609, tel (202) 547-8272. The company researches and reconstructs artifacts, vehicles and vessels of the Viking and medieval period. Two vessels currently in the collection are the 37-ft *Fyrdraca*, a replica 9th century Viking warship, and 20-ft *Gyrfalcon*, a replica 8th century landing boat. The vessels make frequent voyages appearing at waterfront festivals, boat shows and marine exhibits throughout the Chesapeake region. Admission is free at public events. Phone for schedule.

Oxford Maritime Museum, Oxford MD 21654, tel (301) 226-5331. A small volunteer-run museum of local history, focusing on Oxford's role as Maryland's first port of entry. Open from April to mid-October, Fri-Sun 2-5. Admission free.

Pride of Baltimore, Inc., 100 Light St., Baltimore MD 21202, tel (301) 625-5460. The replica Baltimore clipper *Pride of Baltimore* is the city's tall ship ambassador. The *Pride* has a full itinerary, which takes her to various ports all over the world. This is the second *Pride*; the first went down in a tropical squall in 1986. When in port, the vessel is open to the public. Call for schedule.

Project Liberty Ship, Inc., PO Box 8, Long Green MD 21092, tel (301) 661-1550. One of two surviving Liberty ships, the *John W. Brown* on the East Coast represents the "ugly duckling" heritage of these WWII freighters, as the *Jeremiah O'Brien* does on the West Coast. Built in 1942 in Baltimore, she took part in the Anzio landings in 1944 and helped turn the tide of war to victory for the Allied cause. Now undergoing restoration by a volunteer crew, she is expected to be open to the public on a regular basis in Fells Point, Port of Baltimore, in the summer of 1991. Write or call for information.

Susquehanna Museum, PO Box 253, Havre de Grace MD 21078, tel (301) 939-3905. Dedicated to preserving the history of Havre de Grace and the Susquehanna and Tidewater Canal. Call for information.

US Frigate *Constellation*, Pier 1, Constellation Dock, Baltimore MD 21202, tel (301) 539-1797. Commissioned in 1797, the *Constellation* is currently undergoing restoration to return her to her appearance of 1812. Although work is underway, visitors may board the vessel and view exhibits of early Navy artifacts and the ship's history. Open year round, Mon-Fri 10-4, Sat-Sun 10-6. Adults $2.75, Seniors $2, Children $1.50.

MASSACHUSETTS, Salem
Peabody Museum of Salem

To explore the critical role of seaborne commerce in shaping history and culture around the world, to celebrate the diversity and interdependence of cultures and to examine the relationship between people and their environment.

In 1799, twenty-two of Salem's leading overseas traders founded the East India Marine Society in order to share navigational information, provide for the families of those lost at sea and—according to the original charter—"to form a museum of natural and artificial curiosities such as are to be found beyond the Cape of Good Hope and Cape Horn." In those days, Salem was North America's leading port in the East Indies trade, as it had been throughout the 17th and 18th centuries. And by 1821, Yankee skippers had enriched Salem with cargoes of textiles, spices, coffee, tea and finished goods. As this trade with distant civilizations flourished, the Marine Society's collection continued to grow. In 1867 a gift from George Peabody established the collection as the Peabody Academy of Science, and it was later renamed Peabody Museum of Salem. Throughout its history, Peabody has been world-renowned for the depth and breadth of its collections, and it has often held leading roles in worldwide interest in subjects such as Japanese arts and crafts, marine biology, export silver and furniture and marine art. Today the collection is divided among five interconnected subject areas: Maritime History, Asian Export Art, Ethnology, Natural History, and Archaeology.

The museum is located on East India Square at the heart of Salem's historic district. Seven buildings totalling more than 130,000 square feet display over 300,000 artifacts and works of art from the 16th century to the present, in 30 exhibit galleries. Support facilites include a library of more than 100,000 volumes, a photography department with more than one million prints and negatives, and a conservation laboratory for restoring and preserving artifacts. The museum operates on a $2 million budget, with about 100,000 annual visitors, 3,200 members, and 85 employees.

Exhibits: Housed in the East India Marine Hall (built in 1824) and the Dodge and Crowninshield Wings, the maritime history collection numbers some 60,000 objects, including paintings, drawings, prints, ship models, marine

decorative arts, tools, weapons, charts, memorabilia and small craft. These materials range in date from the 17th century to the present day and hail from all over the world—or wherever a Salem ship reached.

USS *Vincennes* exploring Antarctica.

A model of a Salem ship, crafted ca 1750, possibly America's oldest ship model. Below, Nathaniel Bowditch, father of modern navigation.

Exhibits designed around these objects offer the visitor a taste of virtually every aspect of New England's maritime and naval history, focusing on the maritime enterprise that fostered the growth of American commerce and industry, presented within the context of the maritime history of all western civilization. Peabody displays the largest collection of marine art in America, with over 5,000 drawings and paintings including works by William Van de Velde, Winslow Homer, Fitz Hugh Lane, Andrew Wyeth, Antonio Jacobsen and many others. Of special interest are a 21-foot model of the *Queen Elizabeth* originally displayed in Cunard's corporate office lobby, the earliest model of USS *Constitution* (given to the museum by her captain, Isaac Hull), and a Hadley's Quadrant made ca. 1786 for King Louis XVI.

Publications, Programs & Events: Peabody publishes the bi-monthly *Register* which reports on general institutional news, *American Neptune*—the oldest journal of maritime history in the United States, and *The Quarterly Review of Archaeology*. A broad range of educational programs is offered, including guest lectures, film screenings, symposia, tours, visitor interactive demonstrations, courses and an annual antiques show.

Location: Salem is about 12 miles northeast of Boston, reached by Rte. 128 off I95. The museum is on the corner of Essex and New Liberty Streets.
Schedule: Year round, Mon-Sat 10am-5pm, Thurs 10am-9pm, Sun 12-5pm.
Admission: Adults $4, Seniors and Students $3, Children (6-16) $1.50. Members and members of CAMM affiliated museums admitted free.

Membership
Gift Shop
Paid Parking

Peabody Museum of Salem
East India Square
Salem MA 01970
(508) 745-1876
Peter Fetchko, Director

MASSACHUSETTS, Boston
Charlestown Navy Yard/USS *Constitution*
& USS Constitution Museum

The Charlestown Navy Yard preserves structures relating to the founding and growth of the United States and particularly of the US Navy from 1800 to 1974.

The National Park Service presides over 30 acres of the former Boston Naval Shipyard, which was active from 1800 to 1974. The Park is host to Boston Harborfest on July 4th, Harborpark day in mid-September, and *Cassin Young* sea trials on Columbus Day Weekend. US and foreign naval vessels visit throughout the year. A number of structures, vessels and institutions worth mention are maintained on the site:

- USS *Constitution*: Tours by US Navy personnel daily 9:30-3:50.
- USS *Cassin Young* (DD-793): Fletcher-class destroyer, served in the Pacific during World War II.
- Visitor Center (building 5): Audio-visual program on yard history, temporary exhibits.
- Boston Marine Society (building 32): Marine paintings and ship models displayed by society founded in 1747.
- Commandant's House: Home of Navy Yard commandants, 1805-1976.
- Dry Dock #1: Second oldest drydock in the United States, still operable.
- Research collection: Contains artifacts, documents and photographs relating to the Navy Yard and ships associated with it.

USS Constitution Museum

To foster and promote scholarly and popular understanding and appreciation for USS Constitution's *extraordinary role in American history and her current role as a living symbol of this nation's spirit and ideals.*

The Museum was founded as an independant institution in 1972 and opened in 1976. The museum's collections, on 12,000 square feet of exhibit space, contain numerous artifacts, documents, photographs, prints and paintings, along with some 1,000 research books and 50 reels of microfilm.

Exhibits: Permanent exhibits offer background and insight into *Constitution*'s construction, history and preservation, and the lives of her sailors. Designed to supplement a visit and tour of the vessel, the museum's exhibits especially explore the complexity of her design and life onboard, with full-size replicas of her keel, yards and sick bay. Visitors actively participate in many exhibits, computer simulation games, and a video presentation.

Schedule: National Park Service Facilities & USS Constitution Museum: Year round except Christmas and New Year's, daily 9am-5pm.

Admission: Ships and Park facilities: Free.
Museum: Adults $2.50, Seniors $2, Children $1.50.

Boston National Historical Park	**USS Constitution Museum**
Charlestown Navy Yard	Building 22, Charlestown Navy Yard
Boston MA 02129	P.O. Box 1812, Boston MA 02129
(617) 242-5601 John J. Burchill	(617) 426-1812 Caleb Loring, Jr.

The Kendall Whaling Museum

To preserve and provide public access to an international collection of nautical art, history, and ethnology celebrating the human fascination with whales.

De Walvishvangst (the Whale Fishery), by Hendrik Kobell, 1788.

Founded in 1956 around the Kendall family collection begun in 1899, the museum is now operated as a private non-profit educational institution. Its sizeable international collection (70,000+ objects, 15,000 library titles) is maintained and operated by a staff of six, along with volunteers and interns.

Exhibits, Programs, & Events: The Museum's broad scope encompasses the subject of whaling on all seven continents and over a span of more than five centuries. Special to this museum is its coverage of whaling outside that of the United States. This coverage includes unique displays of Japanese scrolls, prints, models and tools, British whaling art, Dutch and Flemish art, numerous Eskimo artifacts, and other tribal art. In addition to a world-famous collection of paintings (including Dutch Old Masters) there is whaling gear from New England, a fully equipped American whaleboat, a Kotzebue Sound Eskimo kayak, and relics from the bark *Wanderer*, the last American square-rigged whaler. The museum offers a full spectrum of programs and services, including films, lectures, tours, monthly members' events, an annual collector's weekend each spring and the Whaling Symposium each October.

Location: Nestled in the wooded hills south of Boston, just off Route 27 near the center of Sharon MA. Approximately 3 miles from exits 8 & 10 of I-95, and about a half hour drive from Boston and Providence.

Schedule: Year round, Tuesday through Saturday 10am-5pm.

Admission: Adults $2, Seniors & Students $1.50, Children $1, Family rate $5, Members free.

Membership
Gift Shop
Picnic Area
Free Parking
Catering

The Kendall Whaling Museum
27 Everett St.
PO Box 297
Sharon MA 02067
(617) 784-5642
Stuart M. Frank, PhD, Director

MASSACHUSETTS, New Bedford
New Bedford Whaling Museum

To collect, preserve, exhibit, and interpret the artifacts and history of whaling in the New Bedford area.

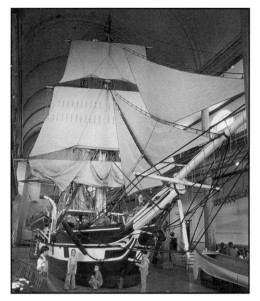

Under sponsorship of the Old Dartmouth Historical Society, the Museum was established in 1903 and is the largest whaling museum in America, with six buildings and over 60,000 square feet of display and storage area. It also houses the resources of a 15,000 volume library and currently has 2,300 members.

Exhibits, Programs & Events: Towering in the great hall, the half-size replica of the *Lagoda* is a fitting centerpiece for the museum. She is typical of the whaleships which sailed from New Bedford in the mid- to late-19th century when it was the country's leading whaling port. Surrounding this model are two preserved whaleboats and an extensive collection of implements and tools of the trade. The museum rounds out the picture of the whaling world with collections and exhibits dealing with shore activity, along with ship models, scrimshaw, photographs and paintings of whaling life and ships, especially in the New Bedford area. Of special interest are two 60-foot sections of the quarter-mile-long "Panorama of a Whaling Voyage" painted in 1848. Arrangements can be made to use the library, which has extensive resources including pamphlets, maps, charts and over 1,100 logbooks.

Location: On Johnny Cake Hill in historic New Bedford, opposite the Seaman's Bethel and a short distance from I-95.
Schedule: Year round, Mon-Sat 9am-5pm, Sunday 1pm-5pm. Sundays in July and Aug 11am-5pm.
Admission: Adults $3.50, Children (6-14) $2.50, Seniors $3. Group rates are available.

Membership
Gift Shop

New Bedford Whaling Museum
18 Johnny Cake Hill
New Bedford MA 02740
(508) 997-0046
Anthony M. Zane, Director

Custom House Maritime Museum

To preserve and protect the maritime history of Newburyport and surrounding communities of the Merrimack Valley.

The Newburyport Custom House was built at the mouth of the Merrimack River in 1835, when the local ports still participated in significant overseas trade. Accordingly, much of the museum is devoted to the port's role in international commerce, and it contains a gallery of interesting foreign objects brought to Newburyport by distant-roaming vessels. Also, as Newburyport was the home of the first US Revenue Cutter *Massachusetts*, there are several displays on Coast Guard History. The Custom House was sold in the early 1900s and turned into a museum in 1975, now with a staff of five and 800 members.

Exhibits: The museum contains an accurate replica of the building's original 19th century Customs office and a room containing models and artifacts representing Coast Guard history. Until 1991, which will be the Service's 200th anniversary, the museum will feature exhibits on Coast Guard history. The museum's annual events include a lecture series, antiques show in March, a flea market in July, dory race in September, Christmas celebrations, and model boat building courses in the winter.

Schedule: April 1-December 20, Mon-Sat 10am-4pm, Sunday 1-4pm.
Admission: Adults $2, Seniors $1.50, Children $1.

Custom House Maritime Museum
25 Water Street, Newburyport MA 01950
(508) 462-8681   Janet H. Howell, Director

Dukes County Historical Society Museums

To preserve the history of Martha's Vineyard and the Elizabeth Islands through museums, libraries, publications, and educational programs.

The Society has two sites on the island, the Jirah Luce House in Vineyard Haven (open summers only), and the Edgartown headquarters, which includes the Thomas Cooke House (open summers only), the Francis Foster Museum, a research library (containing many whaling logs, coastal vessel records and customs records), the Capt. Francis Pease House, and the Gay Head Fresnel lens in use until 1952.

The Foster Museum explores the history of the island with a small collection of artifacts, paintings and models; the Cooke House, built in 1765, held a customs office from 1809-1830 and has several displays on maritime history; the Capt. Pease House contains changing exhibitions. Also on the Edgartown property are a 30-foot 19th century racing whaleboat used in local competitions, and a Nomansland double-ender used by Chilmark farmers for fishing and for transporting sheep to Nomansland in the summer.

Schedule: Summer, Tues–Sat 10am-4:30pm; Rest of the year, Wed–Fri 1-4pm, Sat 10am-4pm.   **Admission:** Adults $2, Children 50¢.

Dukes County Historical Society, Box 827, Edgartown MA 02539
(508) 627-4441   Marian R. Halperin, Director

MASSACHUSETTS, Essex
Essex Shipbuilding Museum

Dedicated to the shipbuilders of the town of Essex, who in their 300-year history have launched over 4,000 two-masted vessels built for the New England fishing industry.

Founded in 1976 and housed in an 1835 schoolhouse, the museum has a small part-time staff, supported by 250 members and a volunteer crew. Museum archives contain ship plans, photographs, and documentation of Essex-built vessels and related industries.

Exhibits & Vessels: Many elements of the shipbuilders craft, including design, lofting, framing, caulking, and in-board joinery are explored in hands-on exhibits. Actual tools, frames, and plans make up the exhibits, enhanced by dioramas, photographs, documents and text. Of special interest are five rigged ship models and fifteen builders' half-models on loan from the Smithsonian Institution's watercraft collection. The auxiliary schooner *Evelina M. Goulart*, built in 1927, will become a permanent exhibit on the nearby banks of the Essex River upon her return.

Schedule: Summer, Thurs-Sunday 11am-4pm. Rest of year by appointment.

Admission: Adults $2, Students & Seniors $1, Children under 12, Residents and Members free.

Essex Shipbuilding Museum
28 Main Street, Route 33, Essex MA 01929
(508) 768-7541   Diana H. Stockton, Administrator

MASSACHUSETTS, Fall River
Marine Museum at Fall River

Only a few hundred yards from the old steamboat pier in Fall River, Massachusetts, is the Marine Museum. Much of the museum's attention is given to preserving the grand memory of the steamboats of the Fall River Line, which operated from that pier on the Taunton River between 1847 and 1937. This is done with the aid of extensive collections of prints, photographs, and memorabilia such as furnishings, uniforms and crockery. The museum also displays an impressive gathering  of over 100 models, many from the famous Seamen's Church Institute collection. Other areas of the history of marine steampower are covered, along with exhibits on knot-tying and nautical crafts.

Schedule: Year round, Mon-Fri 9am-4:30pm, Sat, Sun & holidays 10am-5pm.
Admission: Adults $3, Children (6-14) $2.

The Marine Museum at Fall River, Inc.
70 Water Street, PO Box 1147
Fall River MA 02722
(508) 674-3533   John Gosson, Curator

44

Nantucket Historical Association Museums

To collect, preserve, exhibit, and interpret all manner of artifacts, literature, and documents relevant to the history of Nantucket.

Founded in 1894, the Nantucket Historical Association maintains 11 historic structures on the island (all open to the public). NHA also offers a wide variety of educational services, publishes books on island and whaling history, and maintains a 5,000-volume library and research center adjacent to the Whaling Museum. NHA has 2,600 members, fifteen full-time employees, over six acres of land, and a $1.3 million annual budget.

Exhibits: Displays, furnishings, and settings in the restored buildings portray the way people lived and worked as Nantucket grew from a small farming community to the center of America's whaling industry, to a summer resort. The Whaling Museum is the center of maritime interest, portraying Nantucket's history as the world's busiest whaling port for over a century. Many other aspects of whaling are also presented—techniques and development of whaling worldwide, the men who pioneered the industry, famous ships, and the shoreside industry. Dioramas, large wall maps, ship models, whaling tools, a replica whaleboat, shipsmith's shop, and sail and rigging lofts are incorporated into the exhibits.

Schedule: April 6-June 14, every day 11am-3pm; June 15-Columbus Day 10am-5pm; Columbus Day-24th of Dec 11am-3pm. Closed Christmas-April 5.
Admission: Whaling Museum: Adults $3, Children $1.50; Visitor pass for all sites: Adults $5, Children $2.50.

Nantucket Historical Association, Box 1016, Nantucket MA 02554
(508) 228-1894   Mr. Wynn Lee, Director

Salem Maritime National Historic Site

To preserve and protect the historic wharves and structures from Salem's "Golden Age" of trade, from the Revolutionary War to the early 20th century; and to tell Salem's maritime story to the visiting public and local community.

Established in 1938 and administered by the National Park Service, the site consists of nine acres on Salem's waterfront, encompassing three 18th century wharves and six historic structures from the 17th, 18th and 19th centuries. An 890-piece library and archives have extensive Customs Service documents and records.

Exhibits: The waterfront buildings are preserved with period settings, providing a glimpse into three centuries of Salem's history. The town's role as a major early American port is the focus of exhibits in the Customs House explaining the handling and flow of cargo. Other exhibits explore the local cotton and leather-tanning industries that supplied the town's export trade. Customs equipment, a Customs boat and a wide variety of local furnishings are on display.

Schedule: Year round, every day 9am-5pm. **Admission:** Free.

Salem Maritime National Historic Site
174 Derby Street, Salem MA 01970
(508) 744-4323   Cynthia Pollack, Superintendant

MASSACHUSETTS

Boston Tea Party Ship and Museum, Congress Street Bridge, Boston MA 02210, tel (617) 338-1773. The 110-ft brig *Beaver II*, a former fishing vessel refashioned to resemble an 18th century colonial brig, represents one of the original Tea Party ships. The adjacent museum has displays exploring the political and economic causes and effects of the Tea Party. Costumed guides give tours and in the summer there is a re-enactment of the Tea Party incident. Open year round, daily 9am-dusk. Adults $2.75, Children $1.75.

Cape Ann Historical Association, 27 Pleasant St., Gloucester MA 01930, tel (508) 283-0455. The museum's collection features 38 paintings and 100 drawings by native Gloucester marine artist Fitz Hugh Lane. The Fisheries Collection has schooner models, fishing gear, photographs, log books and journals. There is also a 2,000-volume library on Cape Ann history. Open year round except Feb, Tues-Sat 10-5. Adults $3, Students and Seniors $1.50.

Captain Robert Bennet Forbes House, 215 Adams St, Milton, MA 02186, tel (617) 696-1815. Forbes House is restored to its condition at the end of the 19th century, and it contains displays of ship models, shipboard furniture, marine art prints, drawings and paintings, and other objects from the family collection. Open year round, Wed and Sun 1-4 pm. Adults $3, Seniors & Students $1.50.

Cohasset Maritime Museum, Cohasset Historical Society, PO Box 324, Cohasset MA 02025, tel (617) 383-6930. Housed in a former ship chandlery, this small museum displays shipbuilding tools, paintings, prints and local memorabilia. Call for information.

Donald G. Trayser Memorial Museum, Barnstable Historical Society, Barnstable MA 02630, tel (508) 362-2092. Housed in a former Custom house of 1856, the museum explores Cape Cod's history with an appropriate maritime flavor. Displays include ship models, seafarers' handcrafts, ships' logs and tools. Open July-September. Call for information.

Falmouth Historical Society Museums, PO Box 174, Falmouth MA 02541, tel (508) 548-4857. A museum of local history, it displays paintings, prints and whaling tools. Call for hours.

King Caesar House, Powder Point, Duxbury MA 02332, tel (617) 934-2378. The 1808 mansion of shipbuilding giant Ezra Weston II has been preserved with many authentic furnishings, artifacts, local marine paintings, and photographs. Guided tours are offered. Open mid-June to Labor Day, Tues-Sun 1-4 pm.

Gloucester Schooner Adventure, Harbor Loop, PO Box 1306, Gloucester, MA 01930, tel (508) 281-8079. The 107-foot *Adventure*, built in 1926, is the last American Grand Banks fishing schooner still sailing. Open year round, Tues-Sun, 10-4. Admission is free.

Historical Society of Old Yarmouth, 2 Strawberry Lane, Box 11, Yarmouth Port MA 02675, tel (617) 362-3021. Established to preserve a captain's house and seamen's chapel. Call for information.

Hull Lifesaving Museum, 6 Circuit Avenue, Hull MA 01930, tel (617) 925-5433. Contains exhibits on local maritime history, along with many artifacts from lifesaving establishments in the region. Open Sept-June, weekends only 12-5; July & August, Wed-Sun 12-5. Adults $2, Children $1.

Lightship New Bedford, c/o Harbor Development Commission, Pier 3, New Bedford MA 02740. The 133-foot steel-hulled lightship, built in 1930, is berthed at the town landing and currently undergoing restoration.

Marblehead Historical Society, 161 Washington St., Marblehead MA 01945, tel (617) 631-1069. The 16-room Jeremiah Lee Mansion is open to the public as a monument to the prosperity brought by the sea to Marblehead in the 19th century. A marine room contains displays of sextants, ship's logs, local seafarers' clothing, and parts of small boats. Open for guided tours May to mid-Oct, 10-4 daily. Admission $3.

Massachusetts Schooner Ernestina/Morrissey Museum, 10 Union St., New Bedford MA 02740, tel (508) 992-4900. Launched in Essex MA in 1894, as the *Effie M. Morrissey*, she served three long, distinguished careers: as a Grand Banks fishing schooner, US Navy survey and supply vessel in WWII, and lastly as a packet sailing out of Cape Verde, where she was renamed *Ernestina* in 1948. A small museum exists to preserve and make accessible research materials on 19th century fishing schooners, Arctic expeditions, WWII, Republic of Cape Verde, Portuguese colonialism, Luso-African immigration, trans-Atlantic packet ships, historic restoration, and the African-American contribution to American maritime heritage. Open year round, Mon-Fri 10-3. Museum and Ship Tour $3. Museum Program $1.50.

***Mayflower II*, Plimoth Plantation,** PO Box 1620, Warren Avenue, Route 3A, Plymouth MA 02360, tel (508) 746-1622. The 181-ton, 106-foot *Mayflower II*, built in 1957, is a full-size replica of the original ship which brought the first pilgrims to America in 1620. She is berthed at Plymouth Harbor State Pier, along with a 33-foot shallop, similar to the workboat brought on the original *Mayflower* and used for exploring, fishing and trading. *Mayflower II* is one of the many living-history exhibits at Plimoth Plantation, which primarily consists of a recreated Pilgrim settlement and Wampanoag Indian village of 1627. Open year round, daily 9-5, July & August, 9-7. Admission charge to *Mayflower* only: Adults $5, Children, $3.25.

MIT Museum/ Hart Nautical Collections, 55 Massachusetts Ave., Cambridge MA 02139, tel (617) 253-5942. Focus of the collections is on the technical history of ship and small craft design, construction and propulsion. Displays of ship models arranged to show the evolution of naval architecture and ship construction in the last 1000 years. Other holdings, most of which are not on display, consist of drawings, books, models, photographs, and some artifacts. The display area is open year round, daily 9am-8pm. Collections not on display are open to researchers by appointment, Tues-Fri.

Museum of Science, Science Park, Boston MA 02114, tel (617) 723-2500. A broad maritime collection includes models of ships throughout the ages and artifacts reflecting the technological aspects of seafaring. Call for information.

Nantucket Lifesaving Museum, Polpis Road, Nantucket MA 02554, tel (508) 228-2413. Preserves and displays artifacts, documents and photographs which recount the history, traditions, and operations of the Life-Saving Service, the Lighthouse establishment, the Revenue Marine Service, the Massachusetts Humane Society, and the Coast Guard. Open June 15-Sept, daily 9:30-4:30. Admission $1.

MASSACHUSETTS

SS *Nobska*, Taunton River, Fall River MA; mailing address: c/o Robert Cleasby, 128 Ocean Ave., Cranston RI 02905, tel (401) 467-4007. This coastal steamer of 1925 is currently undergoing restoration, which will include a museum of the steamboat era on board. Open to visitors most Saturdays (except during winter), when volunteer work crews will show visitors around.

Old Harbor Lifesaving Station and **Salt Pond Visitor Center**, Cape Cod National Seashore, National Park Service, South Wellfleet MA 02663, tel (508) 255-3421. The lifesaving station, moved from Chatham to Race Point at the northern end of Cape Cod, contains exhibits from the US Life-Saving Service. The Salt Pond Visitor center, about halfway up the Cape, on Route 6 in Eastham, also exhibits Life-Saving Service artifacts. Open March-Dec, daily 9-4:30, summer, 9-6.

Old State House, The Bostonian Society, 206 Washington St., Boston MA 02109, tel (617)720-1713. The Bostonian Society, the historical society for the city of Boston, maintains the Old State House as a museum of the city's history. Among the articles of maritime interest are ship models, marine paintings, scrimshaw and wood sculptures. Also in the museum's collection, although not currently on display, are marine prints, sailing cards, ship portraits and navigational instruments. A research library contains some information on shipping. Open April 1-Oct 3l, daily 9:30-5; Nov l-March 31, Mon-Sat 9:30-5, Sun 11-5. Adults $1.25, Seniors and Students 75¢.

Pilgrim Hall Museum, 75 Court St., Plymouth MA 02360, tel (508) 746-1620. The nation's oldest continuously operating museum, built in 1824 by the Pilgrim Society of Plymouth in order to exhibit and interpret the history of the Pilgrims and the town they founded. The main maritime exhibit is the preserved lower half of the hull and frame from the *Sparrowhawk*, an ocean-going vessel lost off Cape Cod in 1626. Open year round, daily 9-4:30. Adults $4, Seniors $3.50, Children $1.50.

Sandy Bay Historical Society and Museum, PO Box 63, Rockport MA 01966, tel (508) 546-9533. Explores the heritage of Rockport area. Exhibits in restored houses include ship models and paintings pertaining to local fishing.

Seaman's Bethel, 15 Johnny Cake Hill, New Bedford MA 02790, tel (508) 992-3295. Just down the road from the whaling museum is this functioning church, with a wall listing the names of all local whalemen and fishermen lost at sea.

Seaman's Bethel Chapel and Museum, Ferry Wharf, PO Box 1821, Vineyard Haven MA 02568, tel (508) 693-9317. Small museum of local artifacts and paintings, many left by visiting sailors.

USS *Massachusetts* Memorial Commission, Inc., Battleship Cove, Fall River MA 02721, tel (508) 678-1100. The 35,000-ton battleship USS *Massachusetts* (BB-59) along with the attack submarine *Lionfish* (SS-298), anti-submarine destroyer *Joseph P. Kennedy, Jr.* and PT-boat 796 are all open to self-guided tours. Open year round, 9-4:30 daily. Adults $5, Children $2.75.

Woods Hole Historical Society, Bradley House Museum, Woods Hole MA 02540, tel (508) 548-7270. Located near the Martha's Vineyard Ferry Terminal, Bradley house contains local artifacts and marine drawings and paintings, mainly of small craft. Outside is kept a preserved small catboat, or "spritser."

MICHIGAN, Detroit
Dossin Great Lakes Museum

To preserve and collect the history of steam and sail navigation on the Great Lakes, with special emphasis on the role of Detroit in the commercial and recreational boating field.

Opened in 1960, the Dossin Museum is the marine branch of the Detroit Historical Museum. Its 7,000-square foot building overlooks the Detroit River, a waterway bustling with ships passing through the Lakes.

Exhibits: A few permanent and several changing exhibits explore all facets of Great Lakes maritime history. On permanent display is the smoking lounge from the steamer *Detroit III*, a 71/2-ton restoration project that contains carved English oak and stained glass. A large ship model collection presents the variety of Great Lakes vessels throughout history, all to the same scale—from the first vessel on the Lakes in 1679 to the world's largest sidewheeler of 1912. A continuously running video presentation chronicles the museum's activities and presents a number of underwater videos on shipwrecks. Subjects frequently explored in the changing exhibits are shipyards, shipwrecks, and hydroplane racing on the Great Lakes. The museum's research library is accessible by appointment. The Great Lakes Maritime Institute sponsors and organizes programs for the Museum, including lectures and a model making contest.

Vessels: The hydroplane *Miss Pepsi* raced under the banner of the Dossin family from 1949-1955. She was the first hydroplane to break the 100 mph mark on a closed course.

Location: On the south shore of Belle Isle, in the Detroit River.

Schedule: Year round, Wednesday through Sunday 10am-5:30pm.

Admission: Suggested donation: Adults $1, Children and Seniors 50¢.

Gift Shop
Free Parking

Dossin Great Lakes Museum
100 Strand/Belle Isle
Detroit MI 48207
(313) 267-6440
John F. Polacsek, Curator

Lake Michigan Maritime Museum

Dedicated to Great Lakes maritime preservation and education, to research and restoration as a means to interpreting and preserving maritime history, culture and environment.

The museum occupies a 3,600-square foot interpretive center overlooking the Black River. Also there is the 1,000-volume Marialyce Canonie Great Lakes Research Library specializing in the anthropology of maritime man in Michigan over the entire period of human occupation.

Exhibits & Vessels: Permanent and temporary exhibits tell the story of the building and use of ships on the Great Lakes and explore how the maritime environment has affected regional culture. Ship models, photographs, artifacts and documents contribute to exhibits on native American traditions, commercial and subsistence fishing, shipping, US Life-Saving/Coast Guard Services, US Lighthouse Service, small boatbuilding and recreational boating. Vessels include the 60-ft fishing tug *Evelyn S.*, a native American dugout canoe, a 26-ft motorized surfboat, a 36-ft lifeboat, and assorted rowing craft.

Schedule: Year round; May-October, 10am-5pm ; November-April, 10am-4pm.
Admission: Adults $1.50, Children and Seniors 75¢.

Lake Michigan Maritime Museum, Dyckman Avenue at the Bridge,
PO Box 534, South Haven MI 49090
(616) 637-8078   Ms. Dorris A. Akers, Director

Mackinac State Historic Parks

To preserve and interpret the historical and natural resources of Mackinac State Historic Parks for the enjoyment and enlightenment of the public.

Set around the picturesque Straits of Mackinac, between Lake Michigan and Lake Huron, are Fort Mackinac, Mackinac Island State Park, Colonial Michilimackinac, and Mill Creek. The central theme of all four parks is "Mackinac: Crossroads of the Upper Great Lakes". Of maritime interest is the Revolutionary War sloop *Welcome* and a small marine museum in the Old Mackinac Point Lighthouse on the grounds of Colonial Michilimackinac.

The lighthouse, built in 1892, contains displays on the region's maritime history and a period setting which depicts the domestic life of a lighthouse keeper in the early 1900s. The sloop *Welcome*, berthed nearby at Mackinaw City Marina, is a 55-foot, 45-ton replica of a British sloop of 1775. Costumed guides give tours of the vessel and discuss the history of the area.

Schedule: Marine Museum: mid-May through mid-Oct, daily 9am-5pm. Sloop *Welcome*: June 15-Labor Day, 9am-7pm.
Admission: Museum is free. Admission for *Welcome* is included with Colonial Michilimackinac: Adults $5.50, Children under 12 $2.75.

Mackinac State Historic Parks, Box 873, Mackinaw City MI 49701
(616) 436-5563   David L. Pamperin, Director

MICHIGAN, Sault Ste. Marie
Museum Ship *Valley Camp*

To collect, preserve, conserve, and interpret maritime artifacts relating to the history and culture of Sault Ste. Marie and the Great Lakes region.

The *Valley Camp* is berthed in the Soo Canals (betweeen Lakes Superior and Huron) alongside a small visitor center at the corner of Johnson and Water Streets. Built in 1917, *Valley Camp* is a 550-foot, 11,500-ton straight-deck bulk freighter. She was in service 50 years, carrying ore from Lake Superior to Lake Erie (logging over 3 million miles) untill she was converted into a museum in 1967.

Exhibits: Visitors are free to roam about most of the ship, inspecting her triple-expansion steam engine, forward crew's cabins, engineers' cabins and fully-intact wheelhouse. In her tremendous holds are several models of regional carriers (including a 32-foot model of the *Belle River*), a navigational aids display, marine hall of fame, research library, various paintings, and a memorial to the *Edmund Fitzgerald* (729-ft ore carrier lost with all hands in 1975). Also, surrounding the holds are six 1200-gallon aquariums containing a wide variety of Great Lakes marine life.

Schedule: May 15-June 30 & Sept 1- Oct 15, daily 10am-6pm; July-Aug, daily 9am-9pm. Closed Oct 16-May 14. **Admission** fees available upon request.

Valley Camp, PO Box 1668, Sault Ste. Marie MI 49783
(906) 632-3658   Kevin Marken, Director

MICHIGAN

Great Lakes Shipwreck Museum, Route 2, Box 279A, Sault Ste. Marie MI 49783, tel (906) 635-1742. Call for information.

Great Lakes Naval & Maritime Museum, PO Box 1692, Muskegon MI 49443, tel (616) 944-9117. Currently the museum consists of the submarine *Silversides* and research vessel *Rachel Carson* (converted from a naval gunboat). Both are under restoration. Vessels are open May 1-Sept 30, daily 10-6. Adults $2.50, Children & Seniors $1.50.

Henry Ford Museum and Greenfield Village, Dearborn MI 48121, tel (313) 271-1620. The functioning sternwheel steamboat *Suwanee*, small craft, marine engines and other maritime items. Open year round, daily 9-5.

Huron Lightship, Museum of Arts and History, 1115 Sixth St., Port Huron MI 48060, tel (313) 982-0891. The lightship is berthed on the St. Clair River in Pine Grove Park and is under restoration to become a permanent exhibit of the museum. A gallery features ship models, artifacts from Great Lakes ships and pleasure craft, and a reconstructed pilot house. There are also marine archives and a photo collection. Year round, Wed-Sun 1-4:30. Admission free.

Jesse Besser Museum, 491 Johnson St., Alpena MI 49707, tel (517) 356-2202. A regional museum of art, history, and science for northeast Michigan with many Great Lakes marine photographs, some ship models, and a research library. Open year round, Mon-Fri 10-5, Thurs 10-9, Sat-Sun 12-5. Admission free.

Maritime Heritage Alliance, Clinch Municipal Marina, Foot of Union St., Traverse City; mailing addr: Box 1108 Traverse City MI 40685, tel (616) 941-0850. The museum consists of the 50-ft replica Great Lakes schooner *Madeleine* and a 20-ft replica Mackinac boat *Gracie L.*, which will sail as a school ship in the spring and fall and be a museum of local marine history in the summer.

Marquette Maritime Museum, 300 N. Lakeshore Blvd., PO Box 1096, Marquette MI 49855, tel (906) 226-2006. Housed in the Old Water Works building, the museum explores the maritime history of Marquette and Lake Superior. Exhibits include a 40-ft Coast Guard vessel, Fresnel lens, antique engines and photos. Open Memorial Day-Sept 30, Tues-Sun 11-5. Admission $1.50.

Michigan Historical Museum, 717 W. Allegan St., Lansing MI 48918, tel (517) 373-3559. Among the exhibits on general Michigan history are occasional temporary exhibits on Great Lakes subjects, including lighthouses and lifesaving stations, underwater archaeology and regional shipping. In the collection are a native American dugout canoe and Ausable River guide boat. Extensive archives of photographs, drawings and documents also cover many Great Lakes subjects. Open year round, Mon-Fri, 9-4:30, Sat. l0-4, Sun 1-5. Admission is free.

North West Michigan Maritime Museum, 324 Main St., Frankfort MI 49635, tel (616) 922-1200. Call for information.

Old Lighthouse and Museum, 5295 Grand Lake Road, Presque Isle MI 49777. Exhibits focus on 19th century lighthouse service and seafaring life. Featured are antiques, nautical instruments, tools, ship fittings and hardware, and two Fresnel lenses. Open May 15-Oct 15, daily 9-6. After Labor Day, 9-5.

Rose Hawley Museum, 115 W. Loomis, Ludington MI 49431, tel (616) 843-2001. A maritime exhibit features a 3rd-degree Fresnel lens. A collection for rotating displays includes photographs of lumber barges, car ferries and life saving operations. Open year round, Mon-Fri 9:30-4:30; Summer, Mon-Sat.

Sanilac County Historical Museum, PO Box 158, Port Sanilac MI 48469-0158, tel (313) 622-9946. Housed in a Victorian mansion, this museum of county history currently has one room devoted to marine artifacts. Call for hours.

Sleeping Bear Dunes National Lakeshore, Box 277, Empire MI 49630, tel (616) 326-5134. Resources at this National Park along 70 miles of Lake Michigan include five lifesaving stations, one lighthouse, two port villages, numerous shipwreck sites, and several small craft. A small maritime museum established in one of the lifesaving stations is open from May to October. Admission is free to all sites. Call for information, as schedules vary.

SS *Keewatin*, Blue Star Highway and Union St., PO Box 511, Douglass MI 49406. The 350-ft passenger steamer is furnished and set up as she was when in service. Photo exhibits aboard. Also at the site are the steam tug *Reiss* and sailing fishing boat *Helen McLeod.* Memorial Day-Labor Day, daily 10-4. Adults $3, Children $1.50.

Teysen's Woodland Indian Museum, 415 S. Huron Ave., Mackinaw City MI 49701, tel (616) 436-7011. Primarily a museum of regional Indian history, a small portion is devoted to the maritime history of the upper Great Lakes. Two wooden dugouts, a birch bark canoe and artifacts. Call for information.

MINNESOTA, Duluth
Canal Park Marine Museum

To preserve artifacts and disseminate information on the history of Lake Superior's commercial shipping, the Ports of Duluth and Superior and the role of the US Army Corps of Engineers in developing the region.

The museum was founded and built by the Army Corps of Engineers in 1973, and it is today operated and funded by the Corps' Detroit district. The museum publishes a bi-monthly journal, and gives hourly tours in the summer.

Exhibits & Vessels: The museum's collection of artifacts, ship models, and reconstructions cover a wide array of Great Lakes Maritime History. The evolution of Great Lakes shipping is depicted in a collection of 45 scale models. There are also exhibits on Port of Duluth-Superior historical development, Duluth-Superior shipbuilding, Great Lakes cargoes and commodities, shipboard engineering, history of the Corps of Engineers, Lake Superior shipwrecks, replicas of ship's cabins and a turn-of-the-century pilothouse, and a 30-foot tall fore-and-aft steam engine of 1908. A small collection of vessels includes a 36-foot Coast Guard surfboat, World War II life raft, and assorted skiffs, rowboats and birchbark canoes.

Schedule: Summer, daily 10am-9pm; Spring and Fall, daily 10am-6pm; Winter, Fri-Sun 10am-4:30pm. **Admission:** Free

Canal Park Marine Museum
Lake Superior Marine Museum Assoc., Duluth MN 55802
(218) 727-2497   C. Patrick Labadie, Director

MINNESOTA

***Julius C. Wilkie* Steamboat Museum**, Lee Park, PO Box 1157, Winona MN 55987, tel (507) 454-6880. This wooden sternwheel steamboat houses exhibits on river history with models, steam engines and other bits of machinery and artifacts. Open May-Oct, daily 9-4:30. Adults $1.50, Seniors $1, Children 50¢.

Leif Erikson Restoration Project, Suite 303, Board of Trade Bldg., Duluth MN 55802, tel (218) 722-3644. The 42-ft Viking ship replica which sailed from Bergen, Norway, to Boston then to Duluth in 1926, is now located in Leif Erikson Park. Plans for the vessel include extensive restoration and a permanent photo exhibit alongside. Open free, year round, daily 6-10.

Split Rock Lighthouse Historic Site, 2010 Highway 61 East, Two Harbors MN 55616. The lighthouse overlooking Lake Superior and a large interpretive facility reveal the role of lighthouses and the life of the keepers. Guided tours are offered. Open May 15-Oct 15, daily 9-5; Oct 16-May 14, Fri-Sun 12-4.

Steamer *William A. Irvin*, 350 Harbor Dr., Duluth MN 55802, tel (218) 722-7876. The straight-decker, iron ore carrier *Irvin* of 1937 is berthed on the waterfront behind the Duluth Entertainment Convention Center. She is open for tours with displays aboard. Also berthed there is the fishing/work boat *Sea Bird*. Open May 1-Oct 15, daily 10-6. Adults $4, Children $2.

Biloxi Seafood Industry Museum

A living memorial to the heritage of the coastal communities, dedicated to preserving our history, heritage, and culture, not only for today's citizens and visitors, but also for future generations.

Opened in 1986, the Seafood Industry Museum is housed in 5,000 square feet of a renovated Coast Guard barracks. It is within walking distance of the Point Cadet Marina where the schooner *Glenn L. Swetman* is kept.

Exhibits & Vessels: The museum tells the story of the people, tools, products and technology of the seafood industry, past and present. Among these are exhibits on Biloxi's early fishermen, boats of Biloxi, boatbuilding, marine blacksmithing, and historic Biloxi cuisine. The museum offers live demonstrations of many daily activities of a seafood worker. The museum's traditional topsail oyster schooner *Glenn L. Swetman* makes frequent voyages, participating in educational programs and tourist promotions.

Schedule: Year round, Monday-Saturday 9am-5pm.

Admission: Adults $2.50, Children & Seniors $1.50.

Seafood Industry Museum
PO Box 1907, Biloxi MS 39533
(601) 435-6320   Dr. Val Husley, Director

MISSISSIPPI

***Cairo* Museum**, Vicksburg National Military Park, 3201 Clay St., Vicksburg MS 39180, tel (601) 636-2199. Portions of the Civil War gunboat *Cairo* are on display in the park. The museum displays nearly 1,200 artifacts recovered from the vessel when she was hauled out of the Yazoo River 102 years after her sinking. Models and photographs provide background. Open year round, every day 9-5; Summer, 9-7:30. Admission is free; fee for parking.

Mark Twain Home Foundation, 208 Hill St., Hannibal MO 63401, tel (314) 221-9010. Housed in the boyhood home of Samuel Clemens, the collection focuses on his life and career, including his years on the Mississippi. Photographs and models of steamboats he piloted and other memorabilia are featured. Open daily except Thanksgiving, Christmas and New Year's; Jan-Feb, 10-4; March-Oct, 8-5, Nov-Dec, 9-4. Adults $2.50, Children $1.

USS *Inaugural*, 2241 Edwards, St. Louis MO 93110, tel (314) 771-9911. Berthed at 300 N. Wharf St., *Inaugural* is a WWII minesweeper restored to her original wartime configuration. Open to the public with tours, April-Oct, daily 10-7. Adults $1.75, Seniors $1, Children $1.25.

NEBRASKA, Brownville
Meriwether Lewis Museum

To preserve the unique vessel Capt. Meriwether Lewis *as a symbol of how the mighty Missouri River was tamed, and to exhibit artifacts relating to the river's history and development.*

Given to the state of Nebraska in 1974 and taken over by the private Meriwether Lewis Foundation in 1987, the vessel, which houses several exhibits, is drydocked on the banks of the river in the Brownville State Recreation Area. **Exhibits & Vessels:** The *Lewis'* dredging equipment, steam engines, two-story boilers, and paddlewheels are the Museum's main attractions. The officers' and crews' quarters have been converted into display booths, with exhibits on the prehistoric Missouri River basin, Indian and fur-trading artifacts, and the taming of the river, along with many others. The *Lewis* is a 300-foot steam powered dredge, built in 1932 and operated by the US Army Corps of Engineers until the mid-1960s. She has a steel hull, wooden upper deck, two huge wooden paddlewheels, and three steam engines. In 1989, she was declared a National Historic Landmark.

Schedule: Memorial Day-Labor Day, every day 10am-5:30pm; May & Sept through mid-Oct, weekends only. Closed mid-Oct through April.

Admission: Adults $1, Children (6-12) 50¢, Children five and under free.

Meriwether Lewis Museum, c/o Peru State College, Peru Nebraska 68421
(402) 872-3815   Jerry L. Gallentine, President

NEW HAMPSHIRE

Piscataqua Gundalow Project, PO Box 1303, Portsmouth NH 03810. The replica gundalow *Captain Edward H. Adams* is berthed at a wharf in the Strawberry Banke Historical district (see below). Open May through September, and the rest of the year by appointment.

Port of Portsmouth Maritime Museum & Albacore Park, Market St. Extension, PO Box 4367, Portsmouth NH 03801, tel (603) 436-3680. This developing museum features the submarine USS *Albacore,* open to the public in the park. The maritime museum/visitors center displays memorabilia and artifacts from the *Albacore* and other Portsmouth-built submarines. Open year round, Mon-Fri 9:30-5:30. Adults $4, Seniors $3, Children $2.

Portsmouth Athenaeum, 9 Market Square, Box 848, Portsmouth NH 03801, tel (603) 431-2538. On guided tours, visitors can view several half-lift builders models, a few fully rigged models, and several works of marine art in the Athenaeum's reading room. A research library is nearby at 6-8 Market Square. Open Tues and Thurs 1-4, Sat 10-4.

Strawberry Banke, Marcy Street, PO Box 300, Portsmouth NH 03801, tel (603) 433-1100. Restored and furnished houses (most from the late 18th and early 19th centuries), exhibits of archaeological digs, early tools, 17th and 18th century construction techniques, and numerous gardens comprise this restored village along the Portsmouth waterfront. Of maritime interest are the ship models and carvings of Captain Edward H. Adams and a boatbuilders shop. Open May-Oct, 10-5 daily. Adults $7, Seniors $6, Students 6-17 $4.50.

Twin Lights Historic Site

To preserve the former Navesink Light Station as a public park, museum and historic site—providing visitors with an understanding of the history of the New Jersey Coast and of the importance of the lighthouse to navigation in the lower New York Harbor area.

The Twin Lights Historical Society, founded in 1956, works with the State of New Jersey to preserve the Navesink Lighthouse at the mouth of Navesink River where Sandy Hook begins. This enormous fortress-like structure was built in 1862, used through the turn of the century and converted to a museum/park in 1956. The Society now has 245 members, some of whom provide volunteer assistance to the three State Park employees.

Exhibits & Vessels: A film and several exhibits are devoted to the lighthouse's more-than-100-year history. The Historical Society's collection touches on a number of related sub-themes, including the history of Navesink Highlands, lighthouse technology, piloting and navigation, the US Life-Saving Service and northern New Jersey small craft. The Museum's collection of small craft includes a replica of the Sea Bright Skiff *Fox*—the first boat to be rowed across the Atlantic Ocean—and two Francis Life-Saving Cars from the Jersey Shore.

Schedule: Year round; every day 9am-5pm. **Admission:** Free.

Twin Lights Historic Site
Lighthouse Road, Highlands NJ 07732
(201) 872-1814   Thomas A. Laverty, Curator

NEW JERSEY

Atlantic County Historical Society Museum, 907 Shore Road, PO Box 301, Somers Point NJ 08244, tel (609) 927-5218. A small museum recounts the life of Navy hero Richard Somers, also displaying ship models and shipbuilding tools. There is a research library which contains ships' logs and documents. Next door is the Somers mansion, also open to the public. Call for information.

Canal Society of New Jersey Museum at Waterloo Village, Macculloch Hall, PO Box 737, Morristown NJ 07060, tel (201) 235-8454. The Canal Museum is maintained by the Society at the preserved 19th century Canal Village of Waterloo. The Society collects artifacts, documents, photographs and memorabilia for display in exhbits on New Jersey's two towpath canals. An introductory video on the canals is shown periodically. Open April-Dec; summer, daily 10-6, spring and autumn, daily 10-5.

Cape May Historical Society, Route 9, Cape May Courthouse, Cape May NJ 08210. Located in the pre-Revolutionary John Holmes House, the museum displays all sorts of memorabilia and works of art. A room in the neighboring barn houses the Cape May Point Lighthouse lens and the maritime collection.

Farragut Marine Museum, Russell Hall, Admiral Farragut Academy, Pine Beach NJ 08741, tel (201) 349-4829. On display are old and new nautical instruments and weapons, artifacts salvaged from shipwrecks, models of famous ships, armed forces uniforms and personal items of Admiral Farragut. Highlights among these are a periscope from U-505 and a replica of Admiral Farragut's cabin on the USS *Hartford*. Open Mon-Fri, 8-4. Admission free.

NEW JERSEY

Halve Maen (Half Moon), Suite 1614, 301 North Harrison Street, Princeton, NJ 08540, tel (919) 738-7154. This replica of Henry Hudson's ship, completed in 1989, is a floating maritime museum of the early struggle to settle and colonize the mid-Atlantic area in the 17th century. A permanent homeport for the vessel, which is still being sought, will have a dockside exhibit of 30 illustrated panels telling the history of the mid-Atlantic area known by the Dutch as "Nieu Nederlandt."

Hudson Waterfront Museum, PO Box 1602, West New York NJ 07093, tel (201) 662-1229 or 420-1789. The museum has two vessels on loan from their owners, *Philip T. Feeney,* an 1892 canal tug, and the Lehigh Valley Railroad Barge #79. The museum has developed changing exhibits for various locations on the waterfront, focusing on the River's industrial heyday from 1860 to 1960. It is currently seeking a home for permanent exhibitions.

New Jersey Naval Museum, PO Box 395, Hackensack NJ 07601, tel (201) 342-3268. The Submarine Memorial Ass'n oversees the USS *Ling,* a two-acre memorial park on the Hackensack River, and the Naval Museum. The *Ling* (SS-297) served briefly at the end of WWII and served the rest of her career in reserve training. Museum displays include submarine photos, battle flags, ship and airplane models. Torpedoes, guns, missiles and mines are on display in the park, and a small research library contains naval books and WWII tapes. Open year round, daily 10-4; Dec & Jan, closed Mon & Tues. Adults $3, Children $2.

Ocean City Historical Museum, 409 Wesley Avenue, Ocean City NJ 08226, tel (609) 399-1801. This general-history museum has an exhibit on the wreck of the four-masted bark *Sindra,* just off Ocean City's beaches. Call for hours.

Paterson Museum, *Holland I* and *Holland II*, 2 Market Street, Paterson NJ 07501, tel (201) 881-3874. On display are two of the first successful submarines designed by John Holland in the 1880s. As the first power-driven diving submersibles, they represent a crucial point in the development of underwater technology.

Sandy Hook Museum, Gateway National Recreation Area, PO Box 437, Highland NJ 07732, tel (201) 872-0115. Within the Gateway National Recreation Area are the 85-foot tall Sandy Hook Light (in operation since 1764, it is the oldest operating lighthouse in the United States) and Fort Hancock, which houses the Sandy Hook Museum. Call for information.

Shoal Harbor Marine Museum, Spy House Museum Complex, Wilson Ave., Port Monmouth NJ 07758, tel (201) 787-1807. Overlooking Sandy Hook and Lower New York Bay, the museum displays artifacts, ship models, fishing gear and other artifacts reflecting Port Monmouth's history as a fishing and shipping village. Call for information.

Toms River Seaport Society, 111 Palmeto Drive, Toms River NJ 08753, tel (201) 341-6763. Established to preserve the maritime heritage of Toms River and of the craft indigenous to the area. Call for information.

NEW YORK, New York City
South Street Seaport Museum

Dedicated to the preservation, restoration and interpretation of New York's 19th century seaport, and the maritime history and traditions which made New York the great international center of trade, immigration, culture and finance.

The South Street project originated in the mid-1960s with the vision of a dedicated crew of volunteers "to recreate in the heart of our city the old seaport of New York." On the waterfront was a collection of buildings and piers along South Street on Manhattan's Lower East Side. From the city's beginnings through the early 20th century, it was New York's seafaring heart, a mecca for sailors, merchants, ship chandlers, provisioners and virtually anyone involved in New York's bustling maritime activity. Since its incorporation in 1967, the museum has pursued its vision by restoring and recreating a small part of the waterfront and has assembled one of the largest fleets of historic ships in the world, providing the area's restored and revitalized buildings with a very visible link to their maritime past.

The Seaport encompasses three piers on the East River and seven blocks between Peck Slip and John Street, just south of the Brooklyn Bridge. Today it consists of roughly three main elements: the historic ships, restored buildings, and two large recently-built retail centers—Pier 17 Pavilion and Fulton Market Building. With numerous shops also located in the restored buildings, the Seaport is home to over 130 commercial establishments.

On the upper floors of the Museum Gallery building is the Melville Library, with 8,500 volumes on New York and general maritime history available by appointment. Museum collections include 5,000 general artifacts and over 1,000,000 archaeological artifacts. With 65 full-time employees and 6,500 members, the museum operates on a $4 million annual budget.

Exhibits: Permanent exhibits on many of the ships convey the atmosphere of life and work on board. Other permanent exhibits are located in the Museum Visitors Center on Fulton Street, exploring New York's maritime past. The Museum Gallery on Water Street features changing exhibits illustrating New York's growth from fur-trading post to booming city, and the Norway Galleries in the A. A. Low Building—once a China trader's counting house—contain changing exhibits on New York's maritime heritage.

Restored Seaport Structures: Facing north on Fulton Street, with their steep roofs and tall chimneys, the builings of Schermerhorn Row form the architectural centerpiece of the Seaport. Built in 1811 on speculation by ship chandler Peter Schermerhorn, the row today contains restaurants, a pub and several specialty stores. Also of special interest are the Book and Chart Store, Titanic

Memorial Lighthouse, and the Bowne & Co. Stationers Building on Water Street, which houses a working 19th century print shop. Many other structures within the Seaport have been restored or are under restoration, including the 1849 A. A. Low Countinghouse, 1780 Joseph Rose House, 1807 Jasper Ward Store (now houses the Center for Building Conservation), 1873 Meyers Hotel, and 1907 Fulton Fish Market "Tin Building."

Vessels: The 347-foot steel-hulled four-masted bark *Peking*, the second largest sailing ship in existence, is berthed at Pier 16. Her four-masted design (with a mainmast that reaches skyward 179 feet) represented the utmost in sailing ship technology when she was built in 1911. She served her entire 20 year career in the nitrate trade, bringing coal and manufactured goods from Europe around Cape Horn to Chilean Ports. After 1931 she was converted to a training ship, then purchased by the museum in 1975. She is open for tours and has several exhibits on board along with recreated mates' staterooms, seamen's foc'sle and the sail room. Also worthy of note is a frequent-running film made aboard the ship in 1929 by Captain Irving Johnson. Berthed at Pier 15 is the 293-foot iron hulled full-rigged ship *Wavertree,* currently under extensive restoration. Built in 1885, she sailed for 25 years, performing a variety of tasks, roaming the world to wherever a paying cargo could be found. Dismasted off Cape Horn in 1910 and sold for use as a storage hulk first in Chile, then in Argentina, she remained there until 1968, when she was purchased by the museum.

Today, visitors can get a behind-the-scenes look at the restoration under way. Other historic vessels include the 1893 wooden fishing schooner *Lettie G. Howard*, 1885 iron cargo schooner *Pioneer*, 1908 Ambrose Lightship, 1925 steam ferryboat *Maj. Gen Wm. H. Hart*, and the wooden tugboat *W. O. Decker*.

Activities, Programs & Events: The schooner *Pioneer* and the Seaport Lines' two replica 19th century paddlewheelers, *Andrew Fletcher* and *De Witt Clinton,* offer daily harbor excursions from May through September. Visitors can often observe the work of craftsmen in the Maritime Crafts Center on Pier 15 and in the Boat Building Shop on John Street. Major yearly programs and events include the Mayor's Cup Schooner Race in September, spring launchings in May, and the "Summerpier" concert series in July and August. Daily tours of the historic district and ships, evening lectures, educational programs for school children and weekend family programs are also available.

Schedule: Year round, daily; Oct-May, 10am-5pm; May-Oct 10am-6pm.

Admission: Adults $5, Seniors $4, Students $3, Children under 12 $2. Extra fees for some ships.

Membership	
Gift Shop	**South Street Seaport Museum**
Picnic Area	207 Front Street
Restaurants	New York NY 10038
Paid Parking	(212) 669-9400
Cafeteria	Peter Neill, President

NEW YORK, Blue Mountain Lake
The Adirondack Museum

To collect, preserve, and interpret artifacts and materials related to the history of the Adirondack region, and to encourage historical study of the region.

Overlooking Blue Mountain lake, the museum houses (in 22 buildings) exhibitions on life, work and leisure in the region. It is operated by a staff of 22, with 1,600 members and a library of over 8,000 books, maps and microfilm.

Exhibits & Vessels: The museum's maritime exhibit contains over 200 regional small craft, most housed in their own separate 10,000-square foot gallery. This extensive collection contains a fascinating variety of non-power pleasure craft. Among these are many canoes, skiffs, and guideboats, the likes of which first penetrated the mountains through their scattered waterways. The museum also gives much attention to the tools and techniques which produced these boats, providing year-round lectures and craft demonstrations in the summer.

Schedule: Memorial Day to Mid-October, every day 9:30am-5:30pm.
Admission: Adults $8, Children $5, Seniors $7. Group rates available.

The Adirondack Museum
PO Box 99, Blue Mt. Lake NY 12812
(518) 352-7311   Craig Gilborn, Director

NEW YORK, King's Point
American Merchant Marine Museum

To promote interest in the American Merchant Marine and to foster greater appreciation of the role it has played in the development of our country.

The museum, located in an historic structure on the grounds of the US Merchant Marine Academy, focuses on the evolution of American shipping since WWI. Open since 1979, it has about 450 members and three employees.

Exhibits: In the museum building there are about 40 ship models displayed in nine exhibit areas. Also on display are the Campbell Collection of rare antique navigation instruments, the Hales Blue Ribbon Trophy and special theme rooms for "Gallant Ships" and the tugboat industry. The museum holds three main events each year: Induction ceremonies for the National Maritime Hall of Fame in May, Nathanial Bowditch Maritime Scholar of the Year Award in the fall, and a reunion celebration for alumni of shipping lines.

Schedule: Year-round except July; Tues-Wed 11am-3pm, Sat-Sun 1-4:30pm.
Admission: Free.

American Merchant Marine Museum
USMMA, King's Point NY 11024
(516) 773-5515   Charles Renick, Executive Director

Buffalo and Erie Naval and Servicemen's Park

*To document past military experiences, during war and peace, recognizing the
sacrifices made by men and women who have served in the armed forces.*

On six acres along the Buffalo River, the
park contains a 5,000-square foot museum
and three decommissioned naval vessels. It
has 12 full-time and 30 part-time employees,
and an annual budget of $900,000.

Exhibits & Vessels: The museum building
houses the Jim Gillis collection of models,
navy artifacts and memorabilia. Forty-one
ship models portray the development of the
US Navy from the American Revolution to 1955. A few Air Force and Navy jets,
Army tanks and other military craft are on display outdoors. Moored alongside
are: Cruiser USS *Little Rock*, launched August 1944, converted to a guided
missile cruiser in 1960, flaghip for the 2nd and 6th fleets in the 60s and 70s;
destroyer USS *The Sullivans*, launched April 1943, served in the Pacific and later
in Korea, earning 11 battle stars over her 2-year career; and submarine USS
Croaker, launched in 1943, served in the Pacific and arrived in Buffalo in 1988.

Schedule: April 1-Oct 31, daily 10am-dusk. Open weekends in November.
Admission: Adults $5, Seniors & Youth $3.50. Group rates available.

Buffalo and Erie County Naval and Servicemen's Park
1 Naval Park Cove, Buffalo NY 14202
(716) 847-1773   Richard E. Beck, Executive Director

Cold Spring Harbor Whaling Museum

*To preserve and protect the maritime heritage of Cold
Spring Harbor—once Long Island's second largest whaling port— and to provide for the public the opportunity
to learn about whales, whaling, general maritime history
(both at sea and on shore) and local Long Island history.*

The Whaling Museum Society was founded in1936, with
interests primarily in the town's history as a whaling port
from 1836 to 1862. The museum currently sits on 1.5
acres, with 4,250 square feet of exhibition space and a
1,500-volume research library.

Exhibits & Vessels: The museum's centerpiece is a fully-
equipped 30-foot whaleboat, used on the last voyage of
the Long Island-built brig *Daisy*. The collection boasts
more than 6,000 artifacts, including whaling implements, marine paintings, figureheads, a 700-piece scrimshaw collection, and ship models. Of special
interest are a diorama of 19th century Cold Spring Harbor and a permanent
exhibit documenting the entire history of Long Island whaling. There are films
on whales and whaling, and changing exhibits on local maritime history, with
special events on Sundays and holidays.

Schedule: Year round, 11am-5pm. Open all week in the Summer, closed Mondays the rest of the year. **Admission:** Adults $2, Seniors $1.50, Children $1.

Whaling Museum, Box 25, Main St, Cold Spring Harbor NY 11724
(516) 367-3418   Ann M. Gill, Executive Director

NEW YORK, Amagansett
East Hampton Town Marine Museum

To preserve the cultural heritage of Long Island's South Fork through interpretive exhibits, public education, an oral folklore archive, and collection of artifacts.
The Marine Museum overlooks the Atlantic Ocean from Amagansett, halfway out on the South Fork. Founded in 1966, it is owned and run by the East Hampton Historical Society.
Exhibits tell the story of the region and its 300-year relationship with the sea.
Main floor exhibits illustrate the interaction of history, geography, technological innovation, and folkways which shaped the fisherman's world, using artifacts from the region's first farmer-fishermen, offshore whalers, deep-water fishermen and commercial processing plants of the 19th century. Top-floor galleries contain models and dioramas which explain eight different methods of fishing, along with ecological displays of life in the neighboring ocean and wetlands. There are also exhibits on shipwrecks, lifesaving, and sportfishing. A local catboat, whaleboat and gunning shanty are preserved on museum grounds.

Schedule: July and August, Tues-Sun 10:30am-5pm; June and Sept, Sat-Sun 10:30am-5pm.   **Admission:** Adults $2, Seniors $1.75, Children $1.

East Hampton Historical Society, 101 Main St., East Hampton NY 11937
(516) 324-6850   Karen Hensel, Executive Director

NEW YORK, Syracuse
Erie Canal Museum

Dedicated to the preservation of the Erie Canal, and to telling the great adventure story of the canal's history—the construction and operation of the world's most successful canal.

The museum is run by a non-profit organization originally founded to save the Weighlock Building in downtown Syracuse. It has seven employees and 750 members.

Exhibits: The Weighlock Building is the only building in the world constructed for the sole purpose of weighing canal boats. As the museum's home, it contains a variety of exhibits, including the recreated weighmaster's office, a hands-on history gallery, and a research library open to the public by appointment. In the building's weighlock chamber is the *Frank B. Thomson*, a 65-foot full-size reproduction of a canal line boat, fully accessible to visitors. The museum also runs a number of community events and field trips throughout the year.

Schedule: Year round; Tuesday-Sunday, 10am-5pm.
Admission: Adults $1, Children (under 12) 50¢.

Erie Canal Museum, 318 Erie Boulevard E., Syracuse NY 13202
(315) 471-0593   Vicki B. Quigley, Director

Erie Canal Village

The Canal Village originated in 1973 in the small city of Rome (about 80 miles northwest of Albany), with the operation of a horse-drawn canalboat on a restored section of the Erie Canal. Since then, a number of 19th century buildings have been restored (and some moved from neighboring towns) to recreate a canal-side village. It is also the home of the New York State Cheese Museum.

Exhibits & Vessels: Among the buildings is a Canal Museum which houses a complete exposition of the canal's history, concentrating on its political, social and economic impact. There are also general exhibits on canal development, which use graphics, boat models and a full-size section of a packet boat interior. An orientation slide presentation gives a history of the site from the days of the Durham boats on Wood Creek to the barge canal. The full-size packet boat *Chief Engineer* offers mule-drawn rides along a three-mile section of the canal. Also on the site is "Clinton's Ditch" (the original Erie), and a stone marker showing where the canal's construction began on July 4, 1817.

Schedule: Memorial Day-Labor Day, every day 10:00am-5:00pm.
Admission: Adults $6, Seniors & Youths $5. Children $3. Boatride is $2.

Erie Canal Village, Rome NY 13440
(315) 337-3999   Larry Daniello, Ass't. Director

Hudson River Maritime Center

To educate the public regarding the maritime heritage of the Hudson River and its tributaries, and to increase public awareness of the waterfront and the river environment.

The Maritime Center occupies a long stretch along the banks of Rondout Creek, just upstream from the Hudson. On its 1.3 acres, there are historic buildings and outdoor exhibits of small boats and the steam tug *Mathilda*.

Exhibits & Vessels: Exhibits explore many facets of river life, such as steam transportation, local industries, ice harvesting, bluestone quarrying, and ice yachting. The museum displays ship models, ship ports, small craft, prints, paintings, and photographs in its main buildings. Outside are the 1898 steam tug *Mathilda* and a number of other smaller craft. As part of the Kingston Urban Cultural Park, the museum has a very active schedule of programs, including community workshops, a lecture series, seasonal festivals, and boatrides to the Rondout lighthouse.

Schedule: May–October, weekdays (closed Tues.) 11-5, Sat & Sun 10-5.
Admission: Adults $3, Children (6-12) $1, Seniors $1.50

Hudson River Maritime Center, 1 Rondout Landing, Kingston NY 12401
(914) 338-0071   Kathleen Gray, Director

NEW YORK, New York
Intrepid Sea-Air-Space Museum

A monument to American know-how and spirit, and a tribute to the men and women who pioneered the marine and aviation sciences.

The Museum consists of three naval vessels berthed on Manhattan's West Side Pier 86. The 872-foot aircraft carrier USS *Intrepid* is the museum's centerpiece and houses exhibits on her flight and hangar decks. On the flight deck are 19 former US Navy aircraft—reconnaissance planes, fighters and helicopters, most of them from recent years. The tremendous hangar deck below is divided into five theme halls: *Hall of Honor, US Navy Hall, Pioneer Hall, Intrepid Hall,* and *Technologies Hall.* Exhibits explore the modern Navy, advances in sea, air and space travel, early flying machines, and *Intrepid's* history. They include numerous weapons, aircraft and multimedia presentations. Across the pier are the 418-foot destroyer USS *Edson* and 317-foot guided missile submarine USS *Growler*, both open for tours.

Schedule: Year round, Wed-Sun 10-5, Summer, every day. **Admission:** Adults $7, Seniors $6, Children 6-12 $4, Children under 6, Military and Members free.

Intrepid Sea-Air-Space Museum
West 46th St. & 12th Ave., New York NY 10036
(212) 245-2533   Zachary Fisher, Chairman

NEW YORK, Bronx
Maritime Industry Museum at Fort Schuyler

To educate the public about the role of the maritime industry throughout history and to work for the preservation of that history through support of activities dedicated toward that effort.

The museum is located in historic Fort Schuyler, at the head of Long Island Sound on the Campus of SUNY Maritime College, America's oldest institution of maritime education. Fort Schuyler also houses the Stephan B. Luce Library which has over 75,000 maritime-related titles.

Exhibits & Vessels: The scope of the museum is international, and its main exhibit presents the evolution of seafaring from the earliest period of recorded history through the modern age, aided by numerous sub-exhibits that highlight areas of particular importance in history. Special collections are the Tufnell Watercolor Collection, WPA Art Collection, Maritime College History Collection, Newsprint Collection, Robert G. Herbert Model Collection, O'Donnell Ocean Liner Photo Exhibit, and the Naval Science Historical Collection. The college's 565-foot training ship *Empire State VI*, and the tugs *General Philip Schuyler* and *Raritan* are open for tours.

Schedule: All year except holidays; Mon-Sat 9-4, Sun 12-4. **Admission:** Free.

Maritime Industry Museum at Fort Schuyler
SUNY Maritime College, Bronx NY 10465
(212) 409-7218   Capt. Jeffrey Monroe, Director

Sag Harbor Whaling and Historical Museum

To perpetuate the culture of Long Island in the 18th, 19th and 20th centuries, preserving artifacts that reflect this culture.

Founded in 1935, the Museum is located on the ground floor of an 1845 Greek Revival mansion near the heart of Sag Harbor on the bay side of Long Island's South Fork. The museum has a small library (which contains local documents and ships' logs), 118 members, 4 employees and a $100,000 annual budget.

Exhibits & Activities: The history of Sag Harbor and Eastern Long Island is explored with much attention to the region's whaling industry and the culture that evolved around its maritime and commercial activities. Most displays contain collections of artifacts which relate some aspect of local culture, including scrimshaw, ship models, oil paintings, musical instruments, glassware, clothing, furnishings and myriad other products of local handiwork. Outside are oil try pots and a 30-ft whaleboat. Museum-sponsored activities include crafts fairs, flea markets, historic re-enactments and whaling films.

Schedule: May 15-Oct 1, Mon-Fri 10am-5pm, Sun 1pm-5pm.
Admission: Adults $2, Seniors $1.50, Children 75¢.
Whaling & Historical Museum
Corner of Main and Garden Streets, PO Box 1327, Sag Harbor NY 11963
(516) 725-0770   George A. Finckenor Sr., Director

Skenesborough Museum

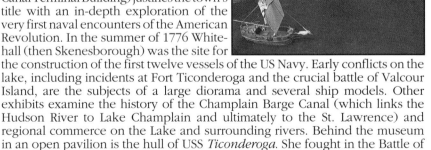

Where the Champlain Barge Canal meets the southern end of Lake Champlain is the town of Whitehall, known as the birthplace of the American Navy. The Skenesborough Museum there (located in the former Canal Terminal Building) justifies the town's title with an in-depth exploration of the very first naval encounters of the American Revolution. In the summer of 1776 Whitehall (then Skenesborough) was the site for the construction of the first twelve vessels of the US Navy. Early conflicts on the lake, including incidents at Fort Ticonderoga and the crucial battle of Valcour Island, are the subjects of a large diorama and several ship models. Other exhibits examine the history of the Champlain Barge Canal (which links the Hudson River to Lake Champlain and ultimately to the St. Lawrence) and regional commerce on the Lake and surrounding rivers. Behind the museum in an open pavilion is the hull of USS *Ticonderoga*. She fought in the Battle of Plattsburg in 1814 and was raised from the lake in 1958.

Schedule: July 1-Labor Day, Mon-Sat 10am-5pm, Sun 12-5pm.
Admission: Adults $2, Seniors $1, Children 50¢.
Skenesborough Museum, c/o Historical Society of Whitehall
Skenesborogh Drive, Whitehall NY 12887
(518) 499-1155   Carol B. Greenough, Director

NEW YORK, West Sayville
Suffolk Marine Museum

Dedicated to the preservation and display of artifacts pertaining to all aspects of the maritime history of Long Island.

Once abounding with oysters and other shellfish, Long Island's Great South Bay saw centuries of thriving maritime activity. Located right on the Bay's north shore in a former carriage house and oyster house, the Suffolk Marine Museum preserves the history of the Bay and Eastern Long Island.

Exhibits: The carriage house (the museum's main building) contains exhibits covering many general aspects of Eastern Long Island history from yacht racing and small pleasure craft to lifesaving and displays of ship models and paintings. The oyster house displays a number of tools from the Bay's greatest industry, explaining all methods of harvesting, cleaning, packing and shipping oysters. Also in the museum complex are the Frank Penney Boatshop and the turn-of-the-century Bayman's Cottage. Two fully restored oystering vessels, the 60-foot schooner *Priscilla* of 1888 and 36-foot sloop *Modesty* of 1923 are berthed at the museum's dock.

Schedule: Year round, Wed-Sat 10am-3pm, Sun Noon-4pm.
Admission: By donation.

Suffolk Marine Museum
Montauk Highway, PO Box 184, West Sayville NY 11796
(516) 567-1733   Roger B. Dunkerley, Director

NEW YORK, Clayton
Thousand Islands Shipyard Museum

To preserve and interpret the history of nautical life and freshwater activity.

The core of the museum's collection is an assemblage of freshwater small craft, one of the largest in the world. These canoes, skiffs, guideboats, launches, and high speed racers, along with marine engines and related artifacts, reflect the nautical heritage of the Thousand Islands (situated in the Western end of the St. Lawrence river). Exhibits examine these boats, their relationship to life on the St. Lawrence, and the people and skills involved in their development. The museum's library and archives contain an extensive collection of books and periodicals relating to these topics. Museum-sponsored programs include an annual Antique Boat Show, in-school classes, a boatbuilding series, and "adventures for children."

Schedule: May 15-June 20, every day 9am-4pm; June 21-Sept 2 9am-4pm.
Admission: Adults $4, Seniors $3, Students (7-17) $1. Group rates available.

Thousand Islands Shipyard Museum
750 Mary St., Clayton NY 13624
(315) 686-4104   Bill Danforth, Director

Canastota Canal Town Museum, 122 Canal St., PO Box 51, Canastota NY 13032, tel (315) 697-3451. The museum is among a collection of restored buildings along the Erie Canal and has displays of artifacts, photographs and models on the local heritage of the canal. Call for hours.

City Island Museum, 190 Fordham St., PO Box 33, City Island NY 10464, tel (212) 885-1600. Among the exhibits on this Island community are a few nautical exhibits, including photographs of minesweepers, shipbuilding and log books of Sandy Hook pilots. Call for hours.

Clinton County Historical Museum, PO Box 332, Plattsburg NY 12901, tel (518) 361-0340. Major maritime exhibit explores naval actions on Lake Champlain in 1812. Numerous artifacts recovered form the lake are on display, along with prints, maps and portraits. Open year round. Call for hours.

Delaware & Hudson Canal Museum, Mohonk Rd, PO Box 23, High Falls NY 12440, tel (914) 687-9311. Exhibits depict life on the D & H Canal, which was in operation from 1828 to 1898. Models of canal boats, photographs, dioramas and artifacts are on display. Open May 30-Labor Day, Thurs-Mon 11-5, Sun 1-5; May, Sept, Oct, weekends only. Adults $1, Children 50¢.

Hudson River Sloop *Clearwater*, 112 Market St., Poughkeepsie NY 12601, tel (914) 454-7673. The 100-ft *Clearwater* and the pilot schooners *Woody Guthrie* and *Sojourner Truth* (based separately in Maplewood NJ) comprise part of a growing fleet of historic replica wooden vessels on the Hudson River. *Clearwater*'s mission involves educating the public about the river's heritage and the natural environment, spearheading numerous efforts to clean up pollution on the river. *Clearwater* is frequently open to the public, especially when she appears at festivals along the river.

H. Lee White Marine Museum, Port of Oswego Authority, East Side Dock, Oswego NY 13126, tel (315) 343-4503. The museum interprets the history of Oswego Harbor and Lake Ontario. Exhibits include models, photographs, maps, reconstructed rooms and an extensive collection of artifacts acquired through underwater archaeology. A small but growing research library contains much information on 19th century Lake Ontario vessels. The museum is restoring the 78-foot, 200-ton Derrick Boat No. 8, built in 1925, to house additional exhibits when completed. Open June, weekends l0-5; July l-Labor Day, daily 10-5; rest of the year by appointment. Admission is free.

Lake George Steamboat Co., Inc. Steel Pier Beach Road, PO Box 551, Lake George NY 12845, tel (518) 668-5777. Replica steamboat offers rides on Lake George, passengers can watch the engine in operation. Call for hours and rates.

Marine Museum of the Southold Historical Society, Soundview Road, PO Box 1, Southold NY 11971, tel (516) 765-5500. The society maintains a small museum on the ground floor of the 1858 Horton's Point Light, overlooking Long Island Sound. Current exhibits contain keepers' logs, old photographs, paintings and various marine artifacts. Plans are to restore the light tower and open it to the public. Call for information.

Montauk Point Lighthouse Museum, RFD#2, Box 112, Montauk NY 11954, tel (516) 668-2544. The 100-ft light tower at Long Island's eastern end has been in service since 1797. Automated in 1987, it is now leased by the Montauk

Historical Society, which has set up displays of Long Island lighthouse photographs and drawings, a Fresnel lens and other aids to navigation, and an exhibit on the constant erosion which threatens the lighthouse. Open Feb-Nov, daily 10:30-6:00. Adults $2, Children $1.

Museum of the City of New York, 1220 Fifth Ave., New York NY 10029, tel (212) 534-1672. Early Dutch explorations are depicted in the Dutch Gallery. Port of New York Gallery features ship models representing many facets of New York City's maritime life and virtually every period of its history. Dioramas, prints and maritime artifacts are on display. Admission free.

Museum of the Franklin D. Roosevelt Library, 259 Albany Post Road, Hyde Park NY 12538, tel (914) 229-8114. Museum galleries contain extensive displays on the lives of Franklin and Eleanor Roosevelt. The special exhibit "America on the Seas" is based on FDR's collections and depict America's naval and maritime history during the age of sail. The exhibit consists of ship models, naval manuscripts, books, posters, photographs and artifacts. Collections are available for research. Year round, daily 9-5. Admission $3.50.

Neversink Valley Area Museum, D & H Canal Site, Box 263, Cuddebackville NY 12729, tel (914) 754-8870. Established to acquire and restore historical sites and artifacts within the Delaware & Hudson Canal region, the museum occupies a blacksmith's house of 1800 near the canal and offers lectures, events and displays on local history. Open Thurs-Sun 12-4. Adults $1, Children 50¢.

New-York Historical Society, 170 Central Park West, New York NY 10024, tel (212) 873-3400. The History of Transportation Gallery in the basement features numerous ship models of many types and periods. Paintings and artifacts throughout reflect the nautical aspects of New York, yesterday and today.

Sea Lion* and SS *Chautauqua Belle, Sea Lion Project, Ltd., RD#1, Sea Lion Dr., Mayville NY 14757, tel (716) 753-2403. The *Sea Lion* is an accurate replica ship built to 16th century methods and design. *Chautauqua Belle* is a replica of a small Mississippi river steamer. Both offer cruises on tiny Lake Chautauqua and are open to the public at their berths. Call for hours.

Snug Harbor Cultural Center, 1000 Richmond Terrace, Staten Island NY 10301, tel (718) 448-2500. An 80-acre National Historic District on Staten Island's North Shore, Snug Harbor once housed nearly 1,000 retired seamen as the country's oldest retirement home for merchant sailors. The site now houses a growing center for the performing and visual arts. Open year round, daily dawn to dusk; weekend tours at 2pm. Admission is free.

Southampton Historical Museum, 17 Meeting House Lane, P.O.Box 303, Southampton NY 11968, tel (516) 238-1612. Exhibits on eastern Long Island history include maritime paintings, logs, account books, shipboard equipment, rigging and outfitting, scrimshaw, whaling artifacts, ship models and shipwreck remains. Call for hours.

Vanderbilt Museum, 180 Little Neck Road, PO Box F, Centerport NY 11721-0605, tel (516) 262-7880. The former summer home of William K. Vanderbilt now houses a maritime museum and planetarium. Open year round, Tues-Sat 10-4, Sun & holidays 12-5. Adults $4, Seniors & Students $3, Children $2.

North Carolina Maritime Museum

Charged with the preservation, research, education, and exhibition of the maritime history of North Carolina.

Established in 1975 and funded by the state Department of Agriculture, the museum is located on the historic waterfront of Beaufort, just west of Cape Lookout. The museum has 18,000 square feet of exhibit space, 15 employees, 1,400 members, a 5,000-volume reference library and $500,000 budget.

Exhibits, Programs & Events: Many facets of North Carolina's maritime past are presented, including privateering, local maritime trades, coastal shipping, and lifesaving. Exhibits display maritime artifacts, navigational instruments, coastal birds, marine life, salt water aquariums, and about 75 ship models. There is an exhibit on the US Life-Saving Service. The Harvey W. Smith Watercraft Center houses traditional boats and a boatshop facility. The museum's Small Craft Program researches and documents traditional boats and boatbuilding methods. Events include a traditional wooden boat show, "Strange Seafood" exhibition, and traditional trades and pastimes exhibition.

Schedule: Year round, Mon-Fri 9am-5pm, Sat 10am-5pm, Sun 1-5pm.
Admission: Free.

North Carolina Maritime Museum, 315 Front St., Beaufort NC 28516
(919) 728-7317   Rodney D. Barfield, Director

NORTH CAROLINA

Chicamacomico Life Saving Station, Chicamacomico Historical Ass'n, Inc., Box 5, Rodanthe NC 27968, tel (919) 987-2203. The station was in service from 1874 to 1954, and its seven buildings are all now under restoration. Photographs and artifacts from the US Life-Saving Service and early Coast Guard, along with photographs of shipwrecks and Cape Hatteras weather conditions, are on display. Research facilities available. Open June-Sept, Tues, Thurs and Sat 11-5; Oct, Sat & Sun 11-5. Admission free.

***Elizabeth II* State Historic Site**, PO Box 155, Manteo NC 27954, tel (919) 473-1144. The 69-ft bark *Elizabeth II* was built to represent the smallest of three ships that brought settlers to Roanoke (the Lost Colony) in 1585. Exhibits at the visitor center illustrate shipboard life, motives for exploration, and the lives of native Americans encountered by Englishmen 400 years ago. A slide show depicts life aboard a 16th century sailing ship and provides a brief historical background for guided tours of the vessel. April 1-Oct 31, daily 10-6; Nov 1-March 31, Tues-Sun 10-4. Adults $3, Seniors $2, Children $1.50.

Fort Fisher Historic Site, PO Box 68, Kure Beach NC 28449, tel (919) 458-5538. Near the remains of the historic Civil War fort is a small museum displaying artifacts recovered from nearby shipwrecks and photos of blockade runners. Call for information.

Hatteras Island Visitor Center, Rte 1, Box 675, Manteo NC 27954, tel (919) 995-4474. Located on Hatteras Island in Buxton, the center tells the history of the outer banks. There are restored keeper's quarters for the Cape Hatteras Light Station and exhibits entitled "The Cape at War" and "The Cape at Play." Call for information.

NORTH CAROLINA

New Hanover County Museum, 814 Market Street, Wilmington NC 28401, tel (919) 341-4350. The museum preserves and interprets the cultural and natural history of the lower Cape Fear region. Of maritime interest is a 17 x 20-foot model depicting the port of Wilmington during the Civil War, accompanied by exhibits on imported goods and the naval stores and cotton industries during the war. The museum also displays numerous dioramas, illustrations and artifacts from the award winning Blockade Runners Museum Collection, which it now owns. Open year round, Tues-Sat 9-5, Sunday 2-5. Admission is free.

USS *North Carolina* Battleship Memorial, Eagle Island, PO Box 417, Wilmington NC 28402, tel (919) 752-1829. The USS *North Carolina* (BB55) has been preserved as a memorial to the 10,000 North Carolinians who died in WWII; as an educational facility with programs on naval history; and as a repository for artifacts from all ships named *North Carolina*. A self guided, audio cassette-assisted tour of the battleship takes approximately 1-2 hours. Photographs, prints and models are on display along the tour route. Open year round, daily 8 to sunset.

OHIO, Vermilion
Great Lakes Historical Society Museum

To record, preserve and interpret for public enjoyment and education the maritime history of the world's largest body of freshwater—the Great Lakes.

The Historical Society's collection is housed in an old mansion overlooking Vermilion Harbor on Lake Erie. Also there is the Metcalf research library—one of the largest collections on the Great Lakes. The Society has 5 paid employees and about 3,000 members.

Exhibits: The museum explores many aspects of the entire history of shipping on all the Great Lakes. The model collection includes ships from the earliest sailing vessels on the lakes to modern thousand-footers. Of special interest is a collection of wreck relics, contemporary paintings, a huge mural of ships on the lakes, and a Fresnel lens. The Society holds two meetings and a model boat show each year.

Schedule: April-Dec, every day 10am-5pm; Jan-Mar, weekends only 10am-5pm. **Admission:** Adults $3, Seniors $2, Children (6-16) $1.

The Great Lakes Historical Society Museum
480 Main Street, Vermilion OH 44089
(216) 967-3467   A.B. Cook, Curator

Ohio River Museum

To collect and preserve artifacts and documents relating to the Ohio River, for the sake of increasing understanding of its impact on our country.

The Museum was founded in 1941 and in 1972 moved to a site along the Muskingum River. The Ohio Historical Society operates the River Museum and nearby Campus Martius Museum of the Northwest Territory. **Exhibits & Vessels:** The museum is housed in three exhibit buildings (totalling 5,000 square feet), each exploring a different theme from the river's natural and human history. Using models, artifacts, maps and illustrations, exhibits cover the river's formation, its aquatic life, man's first contact with the river, the "Golden Age" of the steamboat, shipbuilding, towboats and modern-day problems. A half-hour video presentation details the history of the river steamboat. On museum grounds is a replica 18th century flatboat, 18th century dugout canoe, 1885 rowboat and the pilothouse from *Tell City* of 1885. The 181-foot steam towboat *W.P. Snyder Jr.*, built in 1918, is berthed alongside the museum, open for tours. **Schedule:** March-Nov, Wed-Sat 9:30am-5pm, Sun 12-5pm; May-Sept open every day. *W.P. Snyder Jr.* open mid-April through last weekend in Oct. **Admission:** Adults $3, Children $1.

Campus Martius/Ohio River Museum Complex
601 Second Street, Marietta OH 45750
(614) 373-3750   John B. Briley, Manager

OHIO

Canal Fulton Heritage Society, PO Box 584, Canal Fulton OH 44614, tel (216) 854-3808. The society offers rides on the Ohio & Erie Canal aboard the 60-ft, 22-ton replica canal boat *St. Helena II*. They also sponsor canal-related exhibits in two small local museums. Call for hours.

USS *Cod*, on the lakefront adjacent to the Coast Guard Station in Cleveland OH. The vessel is a property of the Great Lakes Historical Society headquartered at 480 Vermilion St., Vermilion OH 44089-1099, tel (216) 967-3467. Submarine *Cod*, a veteran of seven Pacific patrols, is open to the public as a memorial to all submariners. Open Memorial Day-Labor Day, daily 10-5. Admission is $4.

Fairport Marine Museum, 129 Second St., Fairport Harbor OH 44077, tel (216) 354-4825. This small museum of local maritime history is housed in the 1871 Fairport Harbor Light and keeper's house. Ship models, navigational instruments, life saving gear, photos, paintings and the lighthouse lens are on display, along with the fully-equipped pilot house of the ore-carrier *Frontenac*. Call for hours.

Great Lakes Marine and US Coast Guard Memorial Museum, 1071 Walnut Blvd., PO Box 2855, Ashtabula OH 44004, tel (216) 964-6847. Housed in the former residence of the local lighthouse keepers and Coast Guard commanders, the museum displays models, paintings, artifacts and photos of early Ashtabula Harbor, along with the pilot house from the ore-carrier *Thomas Walters*. Open Memorial Day-Oct, Fri-Sun & holidays 1-5. Admission by donation.

OHIO

Rutherford B. Hayes Presidential Center, Spiegel Grove OH 43420, tel (419) 332-2081. Among the collections are documents and artifacts from the prison ship *Success* and Great Lakes research material, artifacts and photos from the Capt. Hamilton collection. Open year round, Tues-Sat 9-5, Sun, Mon, holidays 1:30-5. Adults $3, Seniors $2.50, Children $1.

Historic Roscoe Village/*Monticello II*, 381 Hill St., Coshocton OH 43812, tel (614) 622-9310. This restored 1830s Ohio & Erie Canal town offers rides on the *Monticello II*, a replica of the first packet boat to dock in Port Roscoe after the canal was completed. Open year round, 10-5.

Piqua Historical Area/*General Harrison*, Ohio Historical Society, 9845 N. Hardin Rd., Piqua OH 45356, tel (513) 773-2522. The 68-ft *General Harrison*, replica of a passenger/freight boat of Ohio's canal heyday, offers mule-drawn rides on the Miami & Erie canal. Five display panels illustrate Ohio canal history. Call for information.

Western Reserve Historical Society Museum, 10825 East Boulevard, Cleveland OH 44106, tel (216) 721-5722. Maritime history of Cleveland and the Great Lakes is explored in the museum's transportation gallery.

SS *Willis B. Boyer* Museum Ship, 26 Main St. (International Park), Toledo OH 43605-2032, tel (419) 698-8252. The 617-ft, 1911 lake freighter and the small museum aboard illustrate the history and value of Great Lakes shipping and recreation. A guided tour of the vessel includes the engine room, all after cabins and forward cabins, the bridge and pilot house. Exhibits include photos and prints of Great Lakes ships and half-hull freighter models from 1850 to the present. Spring and fall, Sat & Sun 10-6; summer, daily 10-6. Adults $3.50; Children $2.50.

OKLAHOMA

Muskogee War Memorial Park, One Port Place, PO Box 253, Muskogee OK 74401, tel (918) 682-6294. The celebrated submarine USS *Batfish* (SS-310), launched in 1943, served in the Pacific theater, earning nine battle stars. She is now open to the public on display in the park. Also there is a small museum which displays all sorts of navy memorabilia. Open Mar 15-Oct 15, Mon-Sat 9-5, Sun 12-5. Adults $2, Seniors $1.50, Children $1.

Columbia River Maritime Museum

To preserve and interpret the rich maritime heritage of the Pacific Northwest, with a special emphasis upon the Columbia River region.

Founded in 1962, the Museum occupies a distinctive, modern 37,000-square foot facility built in 1982. Located on Astoria's historic waterfront, the Museum is operated as a non-profit private enterprise, with a $500,000 annual budget, 1600 members, and 18 employees.

Exhibits, Programs & Events: Exhibits are divided into seven thematic galleries: Maritime Fur Trade and Exploration of the Northwest Coast; Navigation and Marine Safety; Fishing, Canneries and Whaling; On the River; Sailing Vessels; Steam and Motor Vessels; and Naval History. The collection includes boats, artifacts, ship models, charts, historic photographs, and marine art. There is also a 6,000 volume research library available by appointment. The Museum's schedule of events, currently in the process of review, includes Maritime Week in May, coordination with the Astoria Regatta in August, and a Holiday Program in December, along with concerts and performances throughout the year.

Vessels: The Museum's Great Hall houses a collection of restored small craft, including a 36-ft motor lifeboat, a 25-ft motor surf boat, a Bristol Bay boat, and two Columbia River salmon gillnet boats. The lightship Columbia, built in 1950 and now berthed alongside the museum, is maintained in fully operating condition, open to the public during museum hours.

Location: Situated on eight acres along the Columbia River, ten miles inland from the Pacific Ocean and directly on US Highway 30.

Schedule: Year round, every day 9:30am-5:00pm.

Admission: Adults $3.00, Children $1.50, Seniors $2.00. Group rates are available.

Membership
Gift Shop
Free Parking

Columbia River Maritime Museum
1792 Marine Drive
Astoria OR 97103
(503) 325-2323
Jerry Ostermiller, Director

OREGON, Portland
Oregon Maritime Center and Museum

The Maritime Center and Museum is located in Portland's Historic Old Town District, across from Waterfront Park and the Willamette River. The museum building is one of the city's best examples of mid-19th century brick and cast iron architecture.

Exhibits & Vessels: The Museum reflects the region's history in its collections of navigational instruments, ship models, shipwright's tools and other nautical memorabilia. Of special interest are 18th & 19th century sextants and octants, models of regional merchant ships and riverboats, and a display on WWI and WWII ships constructed in local shipyards. A whole section is devoted to the battleship *Oregon*, which was Portland's maritime museum until WWII. The museum recently acquired the sternwheel towboat *Portland* and has undertaken her restoration while displaying a small exhibit on her history. The *Portland* served on the Willamette and Columbia Rivers from 1947 to 1980.

Schedule: Summer, Wed-Sun 11am-4pm; Winter, Fri-Sun 11am-4pm.
Admission: Adults $2, Seniors & Students $1.25.

Oregon Maritime Center and Museum
113 SW Front Ave., Portland OR 97204
(503) 224-7724   Tom McDonald, Director

OREGON

Bandon Historical Society Museum, Historic Coast Guard Station, PO Box 737, Bandon OR 97411, tel (503) 347-2164. Exhibits explore many local history topics, including the maritime life of early Bandon and the Coquille River, coastal shipwrecks, and US Life-Saving Service and Coast Guard operations. Open year round, Tues-Sun 10-4.

Clatsop County Historical Museum, Exchange and 16th St., Astoria OR 97103, tel (503) 325-2563. General history of Clatsop county, with some exhibits on the local fishing and logging industries. Open winter, daily 11-4; summer daily 11-5. Adults $3, Seniors $2.5, Children $1.

Lincoln County Historical Museum, 545 SW Ninth St., Newport OR 97103, tel (503) 265-7501. A maritime room displays general maritime artifacts from the region and contains a small exhibit on shipwrecks. Open winter, Tues-Sun 11-4; summer, Tues-Sun 10-5. Admission free.

Oregon Historical Society Museum, 1230 SW Park Avenue, Portland OR 97205, tel (503) 222-1741. The Historic Ships Gallery conveys the rich maritime heritage of the Northwest Coast. Chronological exhibits highlight explorers and voyages of exploration, along with models and paintings of famous Northwest ships. Call for information.

Philadelphia Maritime Museum

To collect, preserve, interpret and make accessible to the general public and the scholastic community resources relevant to maritime heritage, with particular emphasis on the history of areas influenced by the Bay and River Delaware.

Founded in 1961, the Philadelphia Maritime Museum houses the region's premier collection of maritime artifacts—numbering over 10,000 pieces. The Museum also has 30 regional small craft and a 10,000-volume research library containing photographs, maps, charts, and manuscripts. The Museum is housed in a renovated bank building located in the heart of Olde City. The building has 32,000 square feet of exhibit space. Thirty full-time employees are assisted by a corps of volunteers and interns.

Philadelphia shop sign, polychrome wood, 1875.

Exhibits: The collection is displayed in permanent exhibits and changing special exhibitions which present topics from all periods of maritime history, globally and locally. The main permanent exhibits are: "Man and the Sea," with marine art, ship models, navigational instuments and shipbuilders tools that portray the mariner's world; "Dr. Franklin Sets Sail," a presentation of Benjamin Franklin's maritime observations from his many transatlantic crossings, with a video program on life in an 18th century port city; "Philadelphia's Maritime Mementoes," which highlights the best and most beautiful of the collection, showing the diverse nature of Delaware area maritime artifacts, containing models, figureheads, paintings, small boats, prints, books and photographs. Museum activities include monthly membership programs and lectures, fifteen different educational programs for school groups, traditional boatbuilding classes, launchings, meets, regattas, and group trips. A barge at Penn's Landing houses the museum's "Workshop on the Water," where small boats are constructed and restored and boatbuilding classes are held. It is also the site of an annual small craft exhibition.

Schedule: Year round, Tues-Sat 10am-5pm, Sun 1pm-5pm.
Admission: Museum & Workshop: Adults $2.50, Children $1; Workshop only: Adults $1, Children 50¢.

Membership
Gift Shop

Philadelphia Maritime Museum
321 Chestnut St.
Philadelphia PA 19106
(215) 925-5439
John S. Carter, Director

PENNSYLVANIA, Easton
Hugh Moore Historical Park and Museums

To preserve artifacts, documents and structures which tell the story of transportation and related industrial development during the towpath canal era.

Hugh Moore Historical Park and Museums, Inc. runs the park, Canal Museum and the Center for Canal History and Technology Press. Most of the organization's collection is currently in storage, awaiting the completion of a larger Canal Museum building and a new Museum of the Industrial Revolution. The park extends six miles along the Lehigh River and contains a restored locktender's house and three restored locks.

Exhibits, Vessels, Events: Exhibits in the Canal Museum and locktender's house tell the story of America's canals and the industries and lifestyles they supported from 1792 through 1931. On display are models, photographs and artifacts from every aspect of life on and around canals. The park offers rides on the mule-drawn canalboat *Josiah White* and holds an annual Canal History & Technology Symposium.

Schedule: Year round, Mon-Sat 10am-4pm, Sun 1-5pm. Canalboat Rides: Four times daily from Memorial Day to Sept 30. **Admission:** Museum: Adults $1.50 Children 75¢. Canalboat & Locktender's House: Adults $4, Children $2.

Hugh Moore Historical Park and Museums, Inc.
200 South Delaware Drive, PO Box 877, Easton PA 18044-0877
(215) 250-6700   J. Steven Humphrey, Executive Director

PENNSYLVANIA, Philadelphia
Philadelphia Ship Preservation Guild

Dedicated to the preservation of maritime arts and skills and to the operation and restoration of boats and ships to high standards of seaworthiness and historical accuracy.

Supported by the State of Pennsylvania, the Guild has undertaken a number of restoration projects since its founding in 1972. Located at Penn's Landing, the Guild operates a floating woodshop for maintenance and restoration of its three ships: *Gazela Philadelphia*, *Jupiter*, and Barnegat Lightship.

The 177-foot *Gazela Philadelphia* (ex-*Gazela Primeiro*) was built in Portugal in 1883 and is the world's oldest sailing wooden square-rigger. Having served as a coastwise trader in Europe and later as a Grand Banks dory fisherman, today she is a sail training vessel and Philadelphia's maritime ambassador. The Barnegat Lightship, 129-ft overall, served on Five Fathoms Bank off Cape May, and off Barnegat Inlet between 1931 and 1967. She is fully restored and open for tours. The recently acquired 1902 iron diesel tug *Jupiter* is currently undergoing restoration. Most of the Guild's ships and facilities are usually open to the public, depending on the nature of work in progress.

Philadelphia Ship Preservation Guild
Delaware Avenue & Chestnut Street, Philadelphia PA 19106
(215) 923-9030   Kenneth Meyle, President

PENNSYLVANIA

American Philosophical Society Library, 105 Fifth St., Philadelphia PA 19106, tel (215) 627-0706. A number of unique ship models and instruments are on display with the Society's 247-year-old collection. Call for hours.

CIGNA Museum, 1600 Arch St., Philadelphia PA 19103. Tel (215)241-4894. A small museum documenting the history of the Insurance Company of North America, located in the former INA headquarters. Numerous ship models, paintings, ship portraits, and artifacts are incorporated into displays focusing on marine disasters. Open by appointment.

Erie Historical Museum, 356 West Sixth St., Erie PA 16507, tel (814) 453-1899. Established to promote the study and preservation of collections pertaining to regional and Lake Erie maritime history. Call for information.

Franklin Institute Science Museum/Shipbuilding Exhibit, Benjamin Franklin Parkway at 20th St., Philadelphia PA 19103, tel (215) 448-1200. Much of the Franklin Institute's maritime collection is on display in the large permanent exhibit, "Shipbuilding on the Delaware." Artifacts, photographs, models and visitor-participation displays explore the technical aspects of shipbuilding on the Delaware River. Call for information.

Moshulu, c/o Specialty Restaurants Corp., Chestnut Mall, Penn's Landing, Philadelphia PA 19106, tel (215) 925-3237. This 1904 steel four-masted bark was, until recently, berthed at Penn's Landing with a restaurant and small museum aboard. The vessel is currently undergoing a refit in Camden NJ and may be a sail training and museum ship when complete.

New Hope Barge Company, PO Box 164, New Hope PA 18938, tel (215) 862-2842. Offers hour-long rides on the Delaware Canal aboard four replica 19th century mule-drawn canal boats. Call for hours and rates.

Port of History Museum, Delaware and Spruce Streets, Philadelphia PA 19106, tel (215) 925-3804. Exhibits on Atlantic Coast maritime history over the past 200 years. Open year round, Wed-Sun 10-4:30. Adults $2, Children $1.

US Brig *Niagara*, Flagship Niagara, c/o Erie Chamber of Commerce, 1006 State St., Erie PA 16501, tel (814) 871-4596. The *Niagara*, Commodore Perry's flagship at the Battle of Lake Erie (1813), was raised and restored in 1913. She is currently being rebuilt and restored to sailing condition to serve as Pennsylvania's flagship and goodwill ambassador. Displays interpret the Battle of Lake Erie, the War of 1812, and 19th century naval architecture and seamanship. Hours to be announced; call for information.

USS *Olympia* and **USS *Becuna*,** Penn's Landing, Philadelphia PA 19106, tel (215) 922-1898. The cruiser *Olympia*, commissioned in 1895, is the only remaining vessel of America's "new Navy" of the late 19th century. Most of the vessel is open to self-guided tours, and a small museum aboard displays artifacts and memorabilia from the Spanish-American War. The submarine *Becuna* of 1944 is berthed alongside and is also open for tours. Call for hours.

RHODE ISLAND, Bristol
Herreshoff Marine Museum

To collect, preserve, and display products of the Herreshoff Manufacturing Company and other memorabilia commemorating the unique accomplishments of America's most prolific family of boatbuilders.

Founded in 1971, the museum is located on the site of the Herreshoff Manufacturing Company. In 1990 the museum moved to a 23,000-square foot building, which contains a Hall of Boats, research library, video room, exhibit area, model rooms, and visitor-interactive wind tunnel test.

Exhibits & Vessels: The principle Nathaniel Herreshoff followed in his career of design and production—"that lines of power and speed inevitably flow into forms of beauty"—is visible in extensive photographic displays and a collection of vintage Herreshoff yachts. In a time-line display, the entire story of the Herreshoff company is told, from innovations which embraced every facet of sail and steam vessel construction to their famous America's Cup defenders. Currently in the yacht collection are vessels ranging from 19th century catboats to yachts of the first half of the 20th century.

Schedule: May-Oct, Tues-Sun 1pm-4pm.   **Admission:** $2.50

Herreshoff Marine Museum, 7 Burnside St., PO Box 450, Bristol RI 02809
(401) 253-5000   Michael J. Pesare, Manager

RHODE ISLAND, Newport
Museum of Yachting

To preserve and promote the history of international yachting through educational programs and the preservation, collection and display of boats, art, and literature related to yacht history, construction and use.

Founded in 1980, the museum is located on Fort Adams State Park at the mouth of Newport Harbor. The museum occupies over 11,000 sq ft of exhibit space, along with waterfront property and a boat basin. It has a $500,000 annual budget, 1,500 members, six employees and over 5,000 books.

Exhibits, Vessels and Programs: The museum tells the story of yachts and yachting, presenting the sailors, designers, owners and adventurers who were part of the sport and its tradition. Four main galleries interpret this history: The Mansions and the Yachts, Small Craft Gallery, Hall of Fame for the Single-Handed Sailor, and America's Cup Gallery. The museum sponsors educational programs on offshore navigation, yacht design, yacht surveying, and restoration and repair. Flagship of the collection is Sir Thomas Lipton's J-Class sloop *Shamrock V* (built in 1930). *Cythera* (a 30 square meter), *Try* (an Alden Triangle) and a number of other small craft are kept in the museum's boat basin.

Schedule: May 15-Oct 31, every day, 10am-5pm. Galleries open winter by appointment.   **Admission:** Adults $2, Seniors $1.

Museum of Yachting
Fort Adams State Park, Box 129, Newport RI 02840
(401) 847-1018   D. K. Abbass PhD, Director

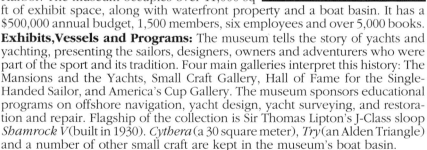

Naval War College Museum

To exhibit and support research in the history of naval warfare and the history of the Navy in the Narragansett Bay region, for the education and edification of the College community, the scholarly researcher and general public.

The Naval War College was established in 1884 "to broaden the officer's views...and give him a just appreciation of the great variety and extent of the requirements of his profession." The College has since greatly expanded and Founders Hall, its original site and since 1964 a National Historic Landmark, now houses the College Museum. The museum has 7,000 sq ft of display area and a 300-volume library.

Exhibits explain the evolution of the "art and science" of war at sea through the centuries and the naval heritage of Narragansett Bay from the Revolution to the present. Special short-term exhibits on Navy-related topics of particular interest to the College also appear during the year. Displays consist of art, artifacts, ship models, weapons, maps and pictorials from the museum's collection and on loan from other depositories.

Schedule: Year round, Mon-Fri 10am-4pm; June-Sept only, Sat & Sun Noon-4pm. **Admission:** Free.

Naval War College Museum
Coasters Harbor Island, Newport RI 02841-5010
(401) 841-4052   Anthony S. Nicolosi, Director

RHODE ISLAND

Providence Public Library, Special Collections, 150 Empire St., Providence RI 02903, tel (401) 455-8000. Eleven ship models of Atlantic Coast fishing craft are displayed in the exhibit room on level B of the library. The special collections room contains ship models, scrimshaw, several harpoons, over 1,000 whaling logs and journals, and over 300 books (many of them rare) on naval architecture, maritime history and model boat building. Call for hours.

Sloop *Providence*, Seaport 76 Foundation, PO Box 76, Newport RI 02840, tel (401) 846-1776. The 110-ft topsail sloop *Providence* is a reproduction of the 1776 merchant/fighting ship which was the first ship commissioned into America's navy, a successful warship with over 40 captures or sinkings to her credit. *Providence* today serves mainly as a sail training or charter vessel and is home-ported in Newport.

SOUTH CAROLINA, Mt. Pleasant
Patriots Point Naval and Maritime Museum

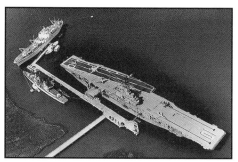

On the eastern side of Charleston's harbor, the Patriots Point Development Authority was established in 1973 to make a home for the aircraft carrier USS *Yorktown*. Today the museum has four more historic vessels: the submarine *Clamagore*, destroyer *Laffey*, nuclear cargo vessel *Savannah*, and USCGC *Ingham*.

Exhibits & Vessels: All five ships are open for self-guided tours, with many working and living areas restored and enhanced with displays. In addition to the displays of artifacts from the naval vessels, there are exhibits of WWII aircraft, national memorials, ship and airplane models, military uniforms, weapons and ammunition, and historic documents. The museum also hosts youth group camping expeditions, and has daily showings of "The Fighting Lady"—the Academy Award-winning film about the *Yorktown*.

Schedule: Year round, every day; Oct-March, 9am-5pm; Apr-Sept 9am-6pm.
Admission: Adults $8, Children (6-11) $4.

Patriots Point Naval and Maritime Museum
40 Patriots Point Road, Mt. Pleasant SC 29464
(803) 884-2727   Charles G. Waldrop, Director

SOUTH CAROLINA

Charles Towne Landing–1670, 1500 Old Towne Rd., Charleston SC 29407, tel (803) 556-4450. The site of the first permanent English settlement in South Carolina is today a state-owned nature preserve and permanent historic site. The ketch *Adventure*, berthed at the park in the Ashley River, is a full-size replica, typical of 17th century colonial vessels. Exhibits in the Interpretive Center include six dugout canoes and other artifacts and displays interpreting the first 100 years of the colony. Call for hours.

The Charleston Museum, 360 Meeting St., Charleston SC 29403, tel (803) 722-2996. A replica of the confederate submarine *Hunley* is on display. The original *Hunley* was used in one of many daring attempts to break the Union blockade of Charleston Harbor. Call for hours.

SOUTH DAKOTA

Battleship South Dakota Memorial, 600 East 7th St., Sioux Falls SD 57103, tel (605) 339-7060. A model of the ship along with several original parts of the vessel are on display in a park dedicated to the men who served aboard her.

Texas Maritime Museum

Dedicated to the collection, preservation, and appreciation of Texas' maritime heritage—from the earliest days of Spanish exploration to on-going fishing and offshore oil industries.

The new Texas Maritime Museum (opened July 1989) is located about 30 miles north of Corpus Christi, on Aransas Bay. The exhibit building has about 2,500 sq ft of display space, with a large outdoor activity area. Its staff of three is supported by volunteers and members; annual budget is $130,000.

Exhibits, Vessels, and Events: Exhibits examine the events, personalities and other aspects of Texas maritime history, such as the Texas Navy, Texas maritime trade and river navigation. The collection contains photographs, models, tools and equipment, marine art, a growing research library, a 29-ft Texas scow sloop, and a Texas-built fishing boat converted to a bay shrimper. The museum participates in a local arts festival in July and Sea Fair in early September.

Schedule: Year round, Wed-Sat 10am-5pm, Sun 12:30-5pm.
Admission: Adults $2.50, Children $1.

Texas Maritime Museum
PO Box 1836, 1202 Navigation Circle, Rockport TX 78382
(512) 729-1271   Jerry Moore, Director

Texas Seaport Museum /*Elissa*

To interpret Galveston's and Texas' maritime history through the living legacy of the Great Age of Sail.

Owned and operated by the Galveston Historical Society, the restored iron bark *Elissa* and some photographic exhibits constitute the museum's current interpretation. The restoration of the *Elissa* was Phase I of the Society's Texas Seaport Museum. Phase II, to be completed in 1991, is an 11,000 square foot shore complex, which will house exhibits on the ships, immigrants, seaports and seaborne commerce in Texas history. There will also be a theater for slide presentations and an observation deck from which visitors can get a first-hand look at the modern port of Galveston.

Elissa's colorful life began in Aberdeen, Scotland on October 28, 1877, when she was launched by Alexander Hall. Eventually sailing under the flags of five different nations, carrying cotton, bananas, coal and lumber, she was rescued in 1974 from the scrapper's torch in a Greek port, with the help of NMHS. Today, after extensive restoration, *Elissa* is berthed alongside the museum building site, and she sails in the Gulf of Mexico each autumn for an annual series of daysails.

Schedule: Year-round, every day 10am-5pm; Summer 10am-6pm.
Admission: Adults $3.75, Students and Seniors $3.25.
Galveston Historical Foundation, 2016 Strand, Galveston TX 77550
(409) 763-1877   Paul De Orsay, Director

TEXAS

Admiral Nimitz Center, 340 Main St., PO Box 777, Fredricksburg TX 78624, tel (512) 997-4379. Several ship models, weapons, documents and other artifacts recall the life of Fleet Admiral Chester W. Nimitz, Commander-in-Chief of the US Naval forces in the Pacific in WWII. There are also exhibits on the war in the Pacific, and outdoors are a Japanese Garden of Peace and the Pacific History Walk, which displays aircraft and small naval craft from WWII. The Center, located in a hotel built by Admiral Nimitz's grandfather, is dedicated to the men and women who served in the Pacific War.

Corpus Christi Museum, 1900 North Chaparral, Corpus Christi TX 78401, tel (512) 883-2862. Along with exhibits on such topics as anthropology, natural history and ethnic heritage, is a large exhibit (4,800 sq ft) devoted to artifacts recovered from two Spanish merchant ships wrecked on the Texas coast in 1554. Objects from the *San Esteban* and *Espiritu Santu* include cannons, anchors, ships fittings, gold, silver and numerous personal items. Sept-May, Tues-Sat 10-5, Sun 1-5; June-Aug, Tues-Fri 10-5, Sat & Sun 10-6. Adults $2, Children 50¢.

Pate Museum of Transportation, PO Box 711, Fort Worth TX 76101, tel (817) 332-1161. On museum grounds is MSM-5, a 57-ft wooden minesweeper which saw service in Vietnam. In the museum are models of modern freighters. Call for hours.

Port Isabel Lighthouse State Historical Structure, Highway 100, PO Box 863, Port Isabel TX 78578, tel (512) 943-1172. This sturdy brick lighthouse was built in 1853, deactivated in 1905, relit in 1952, and today, with its mercury-vapor beam, is still performing as an aid to navigation. Open year round, daily 10-11:30am and 1-5pm. Adults $1, Children 50¢.

Seawolf Park, Pelican Island, PO Box 3306, Galveston TX 77550, tel (713) 744-5043. The submarine USS *Cavalla* (SS-244), which made six patrols in the Pacific during WWII, and the destroyer escort USS *Stewart* (DE-238), a veteran of North Atlantic convoy duty, are open for self-guided tours. Call for hours.

Battleship *Texas*, 3527 Battleground Rd., La Porte TX 77571, tel (713) 479-2411. The 34,000-ton *Texas*, known as the "last of the dreadnoughts" and once the flagship of the US fleet, serves as a floating monument to those who built and served aboard her. Having recently undergone repair and restoration, she is open for self-guided tours and contains a few small displays on naval history. Open summer, daily 10-6; winter, daily 10-5.

Lake Champlain Maritime Museum
Basin Harbor, **VERMONT**

Committed to the preservation and interpretation of the cultural, commercial, technological, and military history of Lake Champlain and the Champlain Valley in order to expand public awareness towards a most important regional and national cultural resource.

Founded in 1984, the museum consists of four buildings located on the eastern shore of Lake Champlain. Maintained by a staff of six, with two boatbuilders on the premises, the Museum has about 500 members and a growing research library.

Exhibits & Vessels: The primary exhibit building is a restored 19th century school house, featuring maritime and archaeological artifacts, historic maps, prints and paintings. Central to the museum's mission is the construction of a full-sized working replica of the *Philadelphia*, a 54-foot Revolutionary War gunboat—scheduled for launching on July 4th, 1991. A new exhibit illustrates the historical context of the Revolutionary War in the Champlain Valley, the construction of *Philadelphia*, and the crucial battle of Valcour Island. In the Small Boat exhibit are an 18th century bateau, a guideboat, various rowboats, canoes and antique motors. Regional programs include a summer lecture series, underwater archaeological projects, small-boat builder's exhibition, and an apprentice shop program involving work on the *Philadelphia*.

Schedule: May 15-Oct 15, Wed-Sun 10am-5pm. **Admission:** Adults $2, Children & Seniors free.

Lake Champlain Maritime Museum, Basin Harbor VT 05491
(801) 475-2317 Art Cohn, Director

VERMONT

Shelburne Museum, Route 7, Shelburne VT 05482, tel (802) 985-3346. The 220-ft steamboat *Ticonderoga* of 1906 has been moved inland from her original home on Lake Champlain and is on display outside the museum. Several nautical items are displayed aboard the vessel and there are a few maritime exhibits in the museum's preserved lighthouse. Call for hours.

VIRGINIA, Newport News
The Mariners' Museum

To advance man's knowledge and understanding of his maritime heritage, the culture of the sea and its tributaries, its conquest by man, and its influence on civilization.

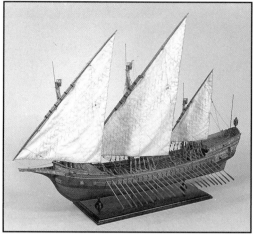

Venetian galleass ca. 1650, Crabtree Collection.

The Mariners' Museum, one of the largest maritime museums in the world, was founded in 1930 by Archer M. Huntington, son of railroad and shipbuilding magnate Collis P. Huntington, who founded Newport News Shipbuilding and Dry Dock Company. The Museum's commitment to preserving and interpreting the culture and lore of the sea is reflected through its extensive collection, five percent of which is on public display in over 64,000 square feet of exhibit space.

Among the collection's 35,000 artifacts are 134 small craft, 800 ship models, 500 navigational instruments, 600 pieces of scrimshaw, 1,300 oil paintings, 1,200 watercolors, and 7,500 prints. Library and archival resources contain 70,000 volumes, 350,000 photographs and one million archival items. The Museum has approximately 100 employees, 120 volunteers, 2,000 members and over 100,000 annual visitors. The main building, with 51,000 square feet of exhibit space, and the new 13,000-square foot Chesapeake Bay Gallery are located in a 550-acre wooded park on the western side of Newport News.

Exhibits: In its galleries, visitors can view artifacts from all over the world, which bring to life countless incidents, developments, and trends in the history of mankind's interaction with the sea. Exhibits incorporate dioramas, audiovisual displays, maps, photographs and small craft—both preserved originals and accurate life-size reconstructions. The Great Hall of Steam, primarily a collection of ship models, presents the evolution and various roles of steamships over 150 years, with displays of artifacts and memorabilia from that age. Directly behind the hall is a collection of figureheads and many other carvings done for, of and aboard all sorts of ships. Two galleries contain permanent exhibits of marine paintings and decorative arts, reflecting the development of marine art from the 17th to 20th centuries. Featured artists include Jacobsen, Bard, Buttersworth, Salmon, Fitzhugh Lane, and Montague Dawson. The Ship Models Gallery explores the complex craft of the ship modeler and the variety of uses man has had for ship models throughout the ages. Another assemblage of models, the Crabtree Collection (considered one of the finest collections of miniature ships in the world), is displayed in its own gallery. Each of these sixteen miniature ships (approx.1:48 scale) was built along original historical lines of construction and finished to intricate detail—each representing an era in the evolution of marine transportation, from a primitive dugout to a transatlantic steamer. A small craft gallery reflects the museum's international scope, displaying vessels from five continents, including a gondola from Italy, canoes from Africa, and sampans from China and Burma. The new Chesapeake

The eagle figurehead from the frigate USS *Lancaster*. At right, the 1870 figurehead from the British bark *Benmore*. Below, woodcarver demonstrates his skill to young visitors.

Bay Gallery contains hundreds of artifacts, photographs, a computer game and maps, which aid in interpreting the history of the Bay, its watermen, shipbuilding and military complexes, navigation, commerce, and recreation. Other galleries highlight pleasure boating and explore the life and work of noted naval architect William Gibbs. Space is also reserved for changing exhibits of timely interest.

Programs, Activities, & Events: Tours by guides (occasionally costumed), historical interpreters, and showings of the movie "Mariner" are conducted daily. The museum has a year-round schedule of special events (almost one a day), including musical programs, feature films and lectures. Members programs feature entertainers, speakers and special travel opportunities. Programs designed for local school systems, children's summer and weekend programs, and adult programs reach over 8,000 participants annually.

Location: Take exit 62A off I-64, 2.5 miles south on J. Clyde Morris Boulevard to Warwick Boulevard.

Schedule: Year round, Mon-Sat 9am-5pm, Sunday Noon-5pm. Closed Dec 25.

Admission: Adults $4, Children (6-16) $1.50, Children under 6 free. Discounts for active military and senior citizens.

Membership
Gift Shop
Picnic Area
Free Parking
Boat Rentals

The Mariners' Museum
100 Museum Drive
Newport News VA 23606-3798
(804) 595-0368
William D. Wilkinson, Executive Director

VIRGINIA, Virginia Beach
Life-Saving Museum of Virginia

To preserve and display the maritime heritage of Virginia as it relates to the Life-Saving/Coast Guard Service, and to encourage research and studies pertaining to the maritime history of Virginia.

Founded in 1981, the museum is housed in the restored 1903 Virginia Beach Seatrack Life-Saving Station. It has a 1500-volume library, 3500 square feet of exhibit space, an annual budget of $200,000, nine staff members, about 60 volunteers, and 600 members. **Exhibits & Events:** Exhibits explore the history of US Life-Saving and Coast Guard services in the region of the Virginia Capes, along with a collection of general-history ship models. Main exhibits tell the stories of the Virginia pilot boats and pilots, the history of the Life-Saving Station, personal histories of surfmen, and the Coast Guard during the war years and today. The museum sponsors numerous special events and programs including a water safety day, small wooden boat show, changing art exhibitions, guest lecturers and musical performances.

Schedule: Year round, Memorial Day-Sept, Mon-Sat 10am-5pm, Sun 12-5pm; Oct-Memorial Day, Tues-Sat 10am-5pm, Sun 12-5pm. **Admission:** Adults $2, Seniors & Military $1.50, Children 75¢. Group rates available.

Life-Saving Museum of Virginia
24th & Atlantic Ave., PO Box 24, Virginia Beach VA 23458
(804) 422-1587   R. Angus Murdoch, Director

VIRGINIA, Norfolk
Hampton Roads Naval Museum

Dedicated to the preservation and exhibition of artifacts, artwork, and memorabilia relating to the rich naval history of the Hampton Roads area.

Founded in 1979, the museum is located on the Norfolk Naval Base, in Pennsylvania House. The building is a two-thirds scale replica of Independence Hall built in 1907 for the Jamestown Tercentennial Exposition.
Exhibits: An in-depth presentation of regional naval history is provided chronologically, highlighting the American Revolution, the Civil War and Gosport Navy Yard, ironclad battles, 1907 Jamestown Exposition, WWII Battle of the Atlantic, development of the modern navy, and NATO. Exhibits contain naval artifacts and artwork, ship and aircraft models, weaponry, underwater artifacts, photographs, ship memorabilia, and a fiber-optic map of the duel between USS *Monitor* and CSS *Virginia*. Tours, lectures and slide presentations are offered.
Schedule: Year round, every day 9am-4pm. **Admission:** Free.

Hampton Roads Naval Museum
Pennsylvania House, Naval Base, Norfolk VA 23511
(804) 444-3827   Elizabeth A. Poulliot, Director

Portsmouth Lightship and Naval Shipyard Museum

On Riverside Park along the shores of the Elizabeth River is the Portsmouth Naval Shipyard and, nearby, the Portsmouth Lightship Museum. The Naval Shipyard Museum preserves and displays artifacts, uniforms, flags, swords, maps and prints, which recall the Shipyard's long history from its opening in 1767 as America's first navy yard to its role in the modern navy. Also on display are a large-scale diorama of Portsmouth in 1776 and models of many famous ships launched at the yard. The Marshall W. Butt library is open by appointment for on-premises naval research. The Portsmouth Lightship, which served for 48 years at various stations along the East Coast, is now a National Historic Landmark, kept out of water and fully restored, with all living and working quarters open to visitors. A growing on-board exhibit on the Coast Guard displays photographs, models, documents, uniforms, and all other sorts of memorabilia.

Schedule: Year round, Tues-Sat 10am-5pm, Sun 1-5pm. **Admission:** All–$1.

Portsmouth Naval and Lightship Museums
PO Box 248, Portsmouth VA 23705   (804) 393-8591

VIRGINIA

Alexandria Seaport Foundation, 100 South Lee St., Alexandria VA 22314, tel (703) 549-7078. Operates the schooner *Alexandria*, a rebuilt Swedish trader of 1929. The vessel is open in port when not cruising the East Coast. Call for hours.

Alexandria Waterfront Museum, Trans Potomac Canal Center, 214 Canal Center Plaza, Alexandria VA 22314, tel (703) 838-4554. This small museum documents the history and operation of the Alexandria Waterfront Canal.

Jamestown Settlement, Rte. 31 South, Glasshouse Point, Williamsburg VA 23185, tel (804) 229-1607. The museum and living history area consists of a recreated Powhatan village, James Fort and three sailing vessels–full-size replicas of the ships that transported 104 settlers from England to Virginia in 1607. Visitors can board the largest vessel, the *Susan Constant*. The *Godspeed* and *Discovery*, built in 1984 to replace older replicas of 1957, are open in the summer and during special events. A replacement for the *Susan Constant* is under construction and expected to be complete in 1991. The museum features an interactive area on ship navigation and ship tools. Open year round, daily 9-5. Adults $5, Seniors $4.50, Children $2.50.

US Marine Corps Air–Ground Museum, Brown Field, Bldg. 2014, Marine Corps Combat Development Command, Quantico VA 22134. Groupings of aircraft, tanks, artillery and weapons, arranged by eras, tell the story of the Marine Corps. Open April-Nov, Tues-Sun 10-5. Admission is free.

VIRGINIA

Watermen's Museum in Yorktown, 309 Water St., PO Box 531, Yorktown VA 23690, tel (804) 887-2641. Displays tell the story of the Virginia watermen and their cultural and economic contributions in eastern Virginia prior to the Revolution. Vessels on view include a Chesapeake dead-rise and a working condition log canoe. Open April-Dec, Tues-Sat 10-4, Sun 1-4. Adults $1, Seniors 75¢, Children 50¢.

Yorktown Battlefield Visitor Center, Colonial National Historical Park, PO Box 210, Yorktown VA 23690, tel (804) 898-3400. The Center's museum interprets the Battle of Yorktown with displays including original arifacts from the land battle and the preceding naval engagement–the Battle of the Capes. In the museum is a full-scale replica of a portion of a British frigate containing recovered cannons. Open year round, daily 8:30-5. Admission is free.

Yorktown Victory Center, Rte 238 and Colonial Parkway, PO Box 1976, Yorktown VA 23690, tel (804) 887-1776. Displays cover the entire American Revolution. An extensive exhibit focuses on the archaeology of the sunken vessels of Lord Cornwallis and includes artifacts retrieved from the river with accompanying explanations of underwater archaeology techniques. Open year round, daily 9-5. Adults $5, Seniors $4.50, Children $2.50.

WASHINGTON, Seattle
Center for Wooden Boats

To operate a living museum preserving and passing on the heritage of traditional small craft.

Founded in 1978 and located in the middle of Seattle on the shores of Lake Union, the Center is a hands-on museum which emphasizes the use of traditional rowing and sailing craft and the learning of heritage boatshop skills. The 2,000-volume library provides information on history, design, reconstruction and voyaging. The Center has 1200 members, a $250,000 budget, three paid staff and a corps of volunteers.

Exhibits & Vessels: Most of the buildings and exhibits are afloat, designed to recreate the true lakeside experience of turn-of-the-century Seattle. An extensive and varied collection of small craft from around the world is maintained afloat and available for public use—dories, skiffs, wherries, canoes, catboats and others ranging from 8 to 35 feet in length. Restoration and new-boat construction, done in a floating 1900s Seattle boat shop, is also part of the Center's presentation. A full calendar of events includes seminars, workshops, speakers, and a three-day Wooden Boat Festival in July.

Schedule: June 15-Labor Day, Wed-Thurs 11am-7pm, Fri-Mon 7am-7pm. Rest of the year: All week (except Tues) 12-6pm. **Admission:** Free, with a small charge to use boats.

Center for Wooden Boats, 1010 Valley Street, Seattle, WA 98109
(206) 382-2628   Dick Wagner, Director

9

Coast Guard Museum of the Northwest

To collect, preserve, and exhibit objects associated with the US Coast Guard in the Pacific Northwest.

Seattle's Coast Guard Support Center on Pier 36 houses the Coast Guard Museum and the Puget Sound Vessel Traffic Center. Also, two 400-foot Polar class icebreakers and two 378-foot high endurance cutters are homeported there. These vessels are usually open to visitors on weekends from 1 to 4:30pm, and the Vessel Traffic Center, on the 4th floor of the main building, is open to visitors from 8am to 4pm daily.

Exhibits: Exhibits in the Coast Guard Museum document the history of the Coast Guard (and the original services from which it was formed—the Lifesaving, Lighthouse, and Revenue Services) in the Northwest, dating back to the 1800s. Displays include ship models, lighthouse and buoy lenses, flags and uniforms, and extensive pictorial displays of ships, aircraft, and Coast Guardsmen. Research facilities contain over 10,000 photographs, 2,000 historical documents and vessel plans, and over 1,000 books and periodicals relating to the Coast Guard and Northwest maritime history.

Schedule: Year round, Mon,Wed, Fri 9am-3pm; Sat, Sun 1-5pm.
Admission: All ships and facilities free.

Coast Guard Museum/Northwest
Pier 36, 1519 Alaskan Way S., Seattle WA 98134
(206) 286-9608

Puget Sound Maritime Historical Society

To collect, preserve, and display objects, relics, and data of maritime interest, with special emphasis on the history of Pacific Northwest maritime activities.

The Museum of History and Industry in Seattle houses the Society's collection, in addition to its own, and displays changing exhibits arranged jointly with the Society. Founded in 1948, the Society has 600 members, a 2,500-volume research collection (open by appointment), a staff of volunteers (aided by MOHAI personnel), and a $50,000 annual budget.

Exhibits are presented in the context of the history of the region and usually consist of photographs, artifacts and ship models. Topics include commercial fishing, tugboats, shipwrecks, sailing ships and construction of the battleship *Nebraska*. New local maritime history and major maritime travelling exhibits (e.g."In Search of the Mary Rose" and "Titanic!") are presented at the museum at least once a year. The Historical Society also has a display booth at Seattle's annual Wooden Boat Fair in July and publishes the quarterly maritime history journal *Sea Chest*.

Schedule: Year round, daily 10am-5pm.
Admission: Adults $3, Children and Seniors $1.50.

Puget Sound Marit. Hist. Soc., c/o Museum of History and Industry
2700 24th Ave. East, Seattle WA 98112
(206) 324-1126   Carl B. Lind, MOHAI Director

WASHINGTON

Bremerton Naval Shipyard Museum, Washington State Ferry Terminal Bldg, Bremerton WA 98310, tel (206) 479-7447. Exhibits, with many ship models, dioramas, photos and drawings, explore some general naval history but mainly focus on the shipyard and its role in WWII. Call for hours.

Edmonds Historical Museum, 118 Fifth Avenue North, PO Box 52, Edmonds WA 98020, tel (206) 774-0900. The museum's Marine Room contains a display of photos (mostly of steamers and ferries), navigational instruments, lights, flags, foghorns and other objects. Twelve ship models and a diorama of the Edmonds waterfront in 1910 are also displayed. Open year round, Tues, Thurs and weekends 1-4. Admission is free, donations are welcome.

Grays Harbor Historical Seaport, 813 E. Heron St., PO Box 2019, Aberdeen WA 98520, tel (206) 532-8611. The Seaport consists of a working shipyard, several exhibits and two wooden sailing vessels. The *Lady Washington* is a replica of the 1780s brig which was the first American vessel in the Pacific Northwest. She currently makes sail training and goodwill cruises and is open to the public when in port. Under separate ownership, the *Columbia Rediviva*, a replica of the same era as the *Lady Washington*, is currently under construction and will serve the same functions. Call for hours.

Naval Undersea Museum, Naval Undersea Warfare Engineering Station, Keyport WA 98345, tel (206) 396-2894. Exhibits cover the history and development of sub-marine vessels and weapons. Call for hours.

Semiahmoo Park Interpretive Center, 8609 Semiahmoo Dr., Blaine WA 98230, tel (206) 332-4777. Exhibits cover the history of the salmon canning industry. A 28-ft Bristol Bay catboat is on display and a film on the Alaska Packers fleet of sailing ships is shown. Call for hours.

Steamer *Virginia V*, 4455 Shilshole Ave. NW, Seattle WA; mailing address: 405 Maritime Bldg, 911 Western Avenue, Seattle WA 98104, tel (206) 624-9119. Launched in 1922, this 125-ft wooden steamboat is the last of the Puget Sound fleet that carried passengers, mail and freight to various ports between Seattle and Tacoma. The vessel makes cruises and is available for charter. Call for information.

W. T. Preston, US Army Dredge, Anacortes waterfront, R. Avenue, Foot of 7th St., Anacortes WA; mailing address: City of Anacortes, PO Box 547, Anacortes WA 98221. This former US Army Corps of Engineers sternwheel dredge of 1928, is now open to the public daily. Call for hours.

Whatcom Museum of History and Art, 121 Prospect St., Bellingham WA 98225, tel (206) 676-6981. The museum's H.C.Hanson Naval Architecture Collection contains thousands of blueprints and drawings, 17 half models and other artifacts and documents relating to the architect's career. Temporary exhibits on regional maritime history are frequently scheduled. Call for hours.

Manitowoc Maritime Museum

To preserve the history of the Upper Great Lakes, and through the study of arti-facts, photographs and documents, tell the story of our past and present cul-ture—of shipbuilding and commerce from sail through steam to today's bulk freighters and pleasure yachts.

The Maritime Museum was founded in 1968 by retired submariners hoping to return a WWII submarine to the city's waters, which were first home to 28 sub-marines during the war. The Museum acquired USS *Cobia* in 1970, and expanded its interests to include Great Lakes maritime history. The Museum has 2,000 members and 15 employees, and—with the addition of a new 8,500 square foot gallery—a total of 21,000 square feet of space in its facility.

Exhibits: The museum's exhibits embrace 140 years of Great Lakes maritime history, commerce, transportation and shipbuilding. The Great Lakes maritime story is told from the earliest era of lakeshore commerce through to the prolific shipbuilding efforts of World War II. Life-size facades of old riverfront buildings recreate a small part of the town in its early days. The model collection includes half-hull, builder's, scale and folk models in the model shipyard. Two movie theaters in the museum show films on WWII shipbuilding, steel shipbuilding and yachting on the Great Lakes. The Museum also provides a research facility, including a 7,000-volume library, along with other archival and photographic collections. Two galleries are reserved for changing exhibits.

Vessels: Submarine USS *Cobia*, launched in 1943 in Groton, Connecticut, saw two years of action in the Pacific, sinking over 18,000 tons of shipping on six patrols. Decommissioned in 1946 and re-commissioned in 1951 for use as a training ship, she was acquired by the Museum in 1970.

Schedule: Year round, daily; May to Sept, 9am-8pm; Rest of year, 9am-5pm.

Admission: Combined (museum and submarine): Adult $5.75, Family $14.75, Children $3.50. Museum: Adults $3.50, Children $2. Group rates available.

Location: Off I-43 on Maritime Drive along the Manitowoc River, about halfway up Wisconsin's coast on Lake Michigan.

Membership	**Manitowoc Maritime Museum**
Gift Shop	75 Maritime Drive
Refreshments	Manitowoc WI 54220
Picnic Area	(414) 684-0218
Free Parking	Burt Logan, Director

WISCONSIN, Sturgeon Bay
Door County Maritime Museums

Door Penninsula extends about 40 miles into Lake Michigan, bordered to the north by a rocky passage known as "Death's Door" (Porte des Morts) and Sturgeon Bay Canal to the south. The region's maritime history is preserved in two museums under common ownership: on the northern end, the Maritime Museum at Gills Rock in the Memorial Park; to the south, Maritime Museum at Sturgeon Bay in Sunset Park.

Exhibits: The Sturgeon Bay Marine Museum is located in the former headquarters of the Roen Steamship Co. Small craft, steamships and marine engines are central themes of the exhibits. Of special interest is a tremendous Dollenberg marine engine, finely-restored launch *Wanda*, and a steamship's pilothouse. Photographs, documents and books also provide information on many aspects of the region's history.

The Maritime Museum at Gills Rock tells some of the many stories of the area's dangerous waters, with artifacts from before the time of LaSalle to the present, many recovered by divers from Door County's waters. Commercial fishing is featured, with a full-size fish tug and 100-year-old ice sled on display.

Schedule: Both museums open from May 26-Sept 3; Sturgeon Bay: daily 10am-4pm; Gills Rock: Mon-Sat 10am-4pm.   **Admission:** By donation.

Door County Maritime Museums
Cana Island Lighthouse, 8820 Cana Island Road, Baileys Harbor WI 54202
(414) 839-2013   Louis Janda, President

WISCONSIN

Hokenson Brothers Fishery, Apostle Islands National Lakeshore, Route 1, Box 4, Bayfield WI 54814, tel (715) 779-3397. Three major structures, the fishing tug *Twilite*, and two open pond net boats have been preserved to represent a small family-operated commercial fishing business in the Apostle Islands region of Lake Superior during 1928-1963. Exhibits cover fish processing, ice harvesting, fishermen's techniques and skills. Open second week in June to Labor Day, daily 9-5. Admission is free.

Great Lakes Marine Collection, Milwaukee Public Library, 814 W. Wisconsin Ave., Milwaukee WI 53233, tel (414) 278-3000. The collection primarily consists of books, periodicals, manuscripts, maps and special files focusing on the history of the Great Lakes. Of special interest to researchers are 10,000 file folders on Great Lakes-related vessels. Open year round, Mon-Thurs 8:30-9, Fri-Sat 8:30-5:30, Sun 1-5.

Portage Canal Society, 528 W. Cook St., Portage WI 53901, tel (608) 742-2739. Two blocks of the canal have been restored in downtown Portage. The Society has no building, but owns some artifacts and photos and maintains exhibits in a few local store windows.

Rogers Street Fishing Village Museum, 2102 Jackson, Two Rivers WI; mailing address: 3415 Tannery, Two Rivers WI 54241, tel (414) 793-2705. Displays tell the story of the first fishing families in the region. Two 1930s fishing tugs, a lighthouse, and shipwreck artifacts are on display. Open June-Aug, daily 10-4. Admission by donation.

SS *Meteor,* Barker's Island, PO Box 775, Superior WI 54880, tel (715) 392-5742. Berthed alongside a replica1890s wharf, *Meteor* is the only remaining vessel of the Great Lakes Whaleback fleet. She has exhibits on board and is open for tours. Call for information.

Head of the Lakes Maritime Society, Marina Drive, Barker's Island, Superior WI 54880, tel (715) 392-5742. Preserves Lake Superior's maritime heritage, with special attention to local history.

CANADA

BRITISH COLUMBIA

British Columbia Provincial Museum, 675 Belleville St., Victoria BC V8V 1X4, tel (604) 387-3701. A museum of general history, it features a full size replica of the stern section of HMS *Discovery* complete with after cabins. Open every day (except Christmas & New Year's) 10-5. Admission free.

Maritime Museum of British Columbia, 28 Bastion Square, Victoria BC V8W 1H9, tel (604) 385-4222. Established in 1954, the museum focuses on early exploration, trading and settlement, with 9,770 sq ft of exhibit space, a 3,700-volume library and an archival collection of over 12,500 photos and documents. The museum's two vessels are the *Tilikum*, an 1850 Indian dugout canoe built on Vancouver Island and later converted to carry sail; and the *Trekka*, a 20-ft. sailboat that completed a global circumnavigation in 1959. Open every day (except Christmas & New Year's) 9:30-6:30, winter hours 9:30-4:30. Adults $4, Seniors $3, Students $1, Children under 6 free.

Vancouver Maritime Museum, 1905 Ogden Ave., Vancouver BC V6J 1A3, tel (604) 736-4431. Located on English Bay, the museum has two historic vessels: the 1880 schooner *Thomas F. Bayard* and the RCMP patrol vessel *St. Roch*, which twice made the passage through Arctic ice from coast to coast in the 1940s. The museum features numerous ship models and other artifacts from Vancouver's maritime past. Open every day (except Christmas & New Year's) 10-5. Adults $1.75, Seniors, Students & Children 75¢.

MANITOBA

Lower Fort Garry National Park, Box 37, Grp 343, RR3, Selkirk, Manitoba R1A 2A8. Tel (204)482-6843. Once an important outpost of the Hudson's Bay Company, the fort houses an original York boat and several recently built replicas of this type widely used by early traders. Open mid-May to mid-Sept, 9-6. Adults $2.50, Children $1.

Manitoba Museum of Man & Nature, 170 Rupert Ave., Winnipeg, Manitoba R3B ON2. Tel (204)956-2830. This general history museum is home to the *Nonsuch*, a 1960s replica of the little ketch that opened Hudson Bay to British traders in 1668. The *Nonsuch* spent several years visiting Canadian ports before coming to her present permanent berth. The vessel has elaborate carvings, common to the period, and may be boarded and visited on guided tours. Surrounding exhibits portray life of the trader and sailor of that era. Open year round. Hours vary; phone for information. Adults $2.50, Students $1.25, Seniors and Children $1.

Marine Museum of Manitoba, Selkirk Park on the Red River, PO Box 7, Selkirk, Manitoba R1A ZB1. Tel (204) 482-7761. Five vessels, some small craft and other maritime artifacts are on display, mostly outdoors. The 151-ft. passenger steamer *Keenora* of 1897 and 150-ft government work boat *Bradbury* of 1915 may be boarded and contain displays aboard. The 80-ft passenger freighter *Chickama II* of 1942, 95-ft fish freighter *Lady Canadian* of 1944, and the 90-ft tug *Pequis II* of 1955 are also on display. Open May through Oct. every day 9-5:30. Adults $3, Seniors & Students $2, Children $1.50.

NEW BRUNSWICK

Albert County Museum, Hopewell Cape, New Brunswick EOA 1YO. Tel (506) 734-2003. This general history museum features many aspects of local life and history including its notable shipbuilding activites, interpreted through photographs, models and artifacts.

Aquarium & Marine Center, CP #1010, Shippagan, New Brunswick E0B 2P0. Tel (506) 336-4771. The emphasis of this center is on the sea life of the Gulf of St. Lawrence, but the museum area features fishing craft and equipment of the area, including the wheel house of a modern fishing boat, and dioramas showing various fishing methods. Open May 25-Sept. 2, daily 10-5. Adults $4, Seniors and Children 6-16 $2.

Grand Manon Museum, Grand Harbor, New Brunswick E0G 1X0. Tel (506) 662-3524. The museum centers on the collection of Walter McLaughlin, lighthouse keeper for 35 years at Gannet Rock. Exhibits feature the island's natural aspects and the fishing and shipbuilding activities at the heart of island life.

New Brunswick Museum, 277 Douglas Ave., St. John, New Brunswick E2K 1E5. Tel (506) 658-1842. This general purpose museum has a large collection of maritime material, including an important collection of ship portraits, a large photo collection and research library. A new permanent maritime gallery is due to open in 1993. Open year round, hours vary, phone for schedule. Adults $2, Students 50¢, Families $4, Seniors & Children under six free.

NEWFOUNDLAND

L'Anse Aux Meadows National Historic Park, PO Box 70, St. Lunaire-Griquet, Newfoundland AOK 2XO, tel (709) 623-2608. This site at the northernmost tip of Newfoundland contains eight foundations believed to be the remains of an 11th century Norse settlement. Visitors may view the archaeological digs and reconstructed sod houses. The Visitors Center presents artifacts and displays that tell the story of the settlement. Write or phone for hours.

Newfoundland Museum, 285 Duckworth St., Beck's Cove, St. John's, Newfoundland A1C 1G9, tel (709) 576-2329. The maritime gallery of this general museum covers Newfoundland's maritime trades of fishing, shaling and sealing. Housed in a waterfront warehouse, the museum displays tools, models, documents and paintings. Open year round, Mon-Fri 9-5, Sat, Sun and holidays 10-6. Admission is free.

Fisheries Museum of the Atlantic, PO Box 1363, Lunenburg, Nova Scotia BOJ 2CO, tel (902) 634-4794. The museum, housed in restored waterfront buildings, has 40,000 sq ft of exhibit space and maintains three large fishing vessels at its dock: the schooner *Theresa E.*

Connor, built in Lunenburg at the Smith and Rhuland Shipyard in 1938; the steel-hulled trawler *Cape Sable*, built in Leiden, Holland, in 1962; and the scallop dragger *Royal Wave*, built in Annapolis Royal, Nova Scotia in 1962. In addition, a number of small fishing boats are on display in the Hall of Inshore Fisheries, including a Cape Island boat, a Northumberland Straits boat and various double-enders and skiffs. Other indoor exhibits include an aquarium and displays on whaling, the Grand Banks fisheries, and sport fishing. Activities include demonstrations of sailors' and fishermen's skills from boatbuilding to canvas work, lobster trap construction and others. Research materials include a 600-volume library, archives, photographs and microfilm. Open May 15-Oct 15, daily 9:30-5:30. July and Aug open to 7pm. Adults $2, Children (5-16) 50¢.

Maritime Museum of the Atlantic, 1675 Lower Water St., Halifax, Nova Scotia B3J LS3, tel (902) 429-8210. Housed in a former waterfront ship

chandlery, the museum focuses on all maritime aspects of regional history except fishing (see Fisheries Museum above), from the renewed Robertson Shipchandlery (the original occupant of the building) to the Navy Gallery, Small Craft Gallery, Age of Steam and Days of Sail galleries. Along with the many ship models, artifacts, photographs and paintings incorporated into the displays, there are over 30 small craft in the collection, including a royal barge and a gundalow. At the museum wharf is the 170-ft hydrographic vessel CSS *Acadia* of 1913, open to the public. The museum offers public demonstrations and programs including oceanography, as well as a conservation lab and research library. Open all year, daily 9:30-5. Closed Mondays from Nov 1-May 14. Admission is free.

Dory Shop, off Route 103, Shelburne, Nova Scotia, Tel (902) 875-3219. At John William's Dory Shop, now returned to its appearance at the turn of the century, visitors can see how dories were made from start to finish. Open July 1-Aug 31, daily 9:30-5:30.

Fisherman's Life Museum, Route 7, Jeddore Oyster Ponds, Nova Scotia, tel (902) 889-2053. This modest home of 1857 has been refurnished to present the life of a rural fishing family. Open May 15-Oct 31, Mon-Sat 9:30-5:30, Sun 1-5:30.

NOVA SCOTIA

John Churchill House, Main St., Hantsport, Nova Scotia BOP 1PO, tel (902) 684-3461. This small collection of paintings, builders models, tools and photographs centers on the ship building activities of the Churchill family and the town of Hantsport. Open July-Sept, 10-noon, 1-5. Admission is free.

Maritime Command Museum, Admiralty House, CFB Halifax, Halifax, Nova Scotia B3K 2X0, tel (902) 427-8250. Located in the former commander's residence near the Navy yard, the museum relates the naval history of the area from the role of the Royal Navy through the World Wars to the present. Uniforms, models, paintings, photos and memorabilia enliven the displays in 15,000 sq ft of exhibit space. Archives and a 30,000-volume library are available for research (phone ahead, please). Open year round, weekdays 9:30-3:30; July and Aug, also open weekends 1-5. Admission is free.

O'Dell Inn & Tavern Museum, Lower St. George St., Annapolis Royal, Nova Scotia BOS 1AO, tel (902) 532-2041. This building once faced the shipyards on which Annapolis Royal thrived. Now restored, it houses a small collection of photographs, artifacts and models. Open June 1-Sept 7, daily 9:30-5.

HMCS *Sackville*, foot of Sackville St., Halifax; mailing addr: Fleet Mail Office, Halifax, Nova Scotia B3K 2XO, tel (902) 429-2132. Her Majesty's Canadian Ship *Sackville* is one of the 123 Corvettes built in Canada for convoy duty in WWII. The vessel is berthed a short walk from the Maritime Museum of the Atlantic (see above), but is separately maintained by volunteers as a National Naval Memorial and is supported by public contributions. Open June-Oct, Mon-Sat 10-5, Sun 1-5. Admission is free, but donations are welcome.

Yarmouth County Museum, 22 Collins St., Yarmouth, Nova Scotia B5A 4B1, tel (902) 742-5539. This small local history museum is overwhelmingly maritime in content, as Yarmouth was once Canada's leading shipbuilding and shipowning center. Housed in a former church, the collection contains wreck remains, models, navigational instruments, documents, photos and a large and significant collection of ship portraits. Archives contain newspapers, letters, diaries, bills of lading and more. Open year round; summer, Mon-Sat 9-5, Sun 1-5; winter, Tues-Sat 2-5. Adults $1, Students 50¢, Children 25¢.

ONTARIO

Collingwood Museum, Memorial Park, St. Paul St., Box 556, Collingwood, Ontario L9Y 4B2, Tel (705) 445-4811. Small museum on the considerable maritime history of the town. Exhibits and holdings include shipbuilding documents, ledgers, letter books, shipbuilding tools, 2,000 photos, a collection of models that includes the distinctive Collingwood skiff, and two reconstructed wheel houses. Collingwood was also the terminus for slaves escaping the South through the Underground Railroad via grain schooners, as recorded in the library of oral histories. Open May 24 to 2nd Monday in October (Canadian Thanksgiving), Mon-Sat 10-5, Sun 12-4. Closed Easter and Christmas. Adults 50¢, Children 25¢.

HMCS *Haida*, Ontario Place, 955 Lakeshore Blvd. West, Toronto, Ontario M6K 3B9, tel (416) 965-7711. This Canadian *Tribal*-class destroyer is a veteran of WWII, in which she was in on the sinking of 14 enemy ships, including four destroyers and a submarine. She also served two tours of combat duty in the

Korean War. She is currently berthed at the Toronto waterfront at Ontario Place, a 96-acre cultural/leisure complex on three man-made islands. Open mid-May to the weekend after Labor Day, daily 10-7. Admission includes the ship and museum and any events in the park. Adults $7, Children $3, Seniors $3.

Hamilton/Scourge Project, Hamilton City Hall, 71 Main Street West, Hamilton, Ontario L8N 3T4, tel (416) 526-4601. Two American schooners lost 175 years ago in a squall on Lake Ontario, are the subject of this archaeological project. The project's Interpretation Center offers an audio-visual program, displays and printed material describing the two ships. Open July-Labor Day, daily 10-6. Admission is free.

Huronia Historic Parks, PO Box 1800, Penetanguishene, Ontario L0K 1P0, tel (705) 549-8064. This 35-acre site, formerly a naval dockyard and military complex, contains 15 reconstructed buildings and a collection of local and period vessels. Costumed staff invite visitors to participate in activities such as sailing programs, musket drills and demonstrations of dockyard and 19th century domestic skills. The park is home to a fleet of historic replica vessels, including two bateaux, a gig, a 14-ft skiff and the schooner *Bee*, replica of the original vessel of 1817. All are operational and used in visitor programs. Open May-early Sept, daily 10-5. Adults $5, Seniors $2.50, Students $3.

Huronia Museum, Ltd., PO Box 638, Midland, Ontario L4R 4P4, tel (705) 526-2844. Artifacts from the area's shipping and shipbuilding activities include an impressive photo collection of Great Lakes shipping, ship models and a double ship's wheel from the steamer *Midland City*. Open May 24-Canadian Thanksgiving (2nd Mon in Oct), Mon-Sat 9:30-5:30, Sun 11-5:30. Adults $4, Seniors $3.50, Students $3.

Marine Museum of the Great Lakes at Kingston, 55 Ontario St., Kingston, Ontario K7L 2Y2, tel (613) 542-2261. Located on the waterfront of Lake Ontario, the museum offers displays of artifacts and models, a library and archives and educational programs. Moored nearby is the 3,000-ton former 1958 icebreaker *Alexander Henry*, now a museum ship and, in the summer, a bed-and-breakfast inn for visitors. A drydock, next to the museum building, is a Canadian National Historic Site. Open April-Oct, daily 10-5; Nov 1 to mid-Dec, Tues-Sun 10-4. Call or write for admission charges.

Marine Museum of Upper Canada, Stanley Barracks, Exhibition Place, Toronto, Ontario M6K 3C3, tel (416) 392-6827. Located on the Toronto waterfront, the museum's galleries explore such topics as warships, submarines, small craft and the fur trade. Exhibits include a 1928 radio room, a fur trader's shop, ship models, steam whistles and more. On the museum grounds is the tug *Ned Hanlan*, open to the public. Open year round, daily Mon-Sat 9:30-5, Sun & holidays 12-5. Adults $1.50, Seniors and Children $1.

Moore Museum, 94 William St., Mooretown, Ontario N0N 1M0, tel (519) 867-2020. Five buildings on 2 acres exhibit topics of local maritime history through photos, instruments, artifacts and special events. Open Mar 1-Nov 30, Wed-Sun 11-5. Adults $2, Seniors & Students $1.50, Children 75¢, Families $5.

Museum Ship *Norgoma*, 99 Foster Dr., Sault Ste. Marie, Ontario P6A 5X6, tel (705) 949-9111. The *Norgoma* of 1950 was the last passenger cruise ship built on the Great Lakes and is now berthed at Sault Ste. Marie with onboard exhibits

ONTARIO

on the ship's career and the Great Lakes area. Adults $2.50, Seniors & Youth $2. Call for hours.

Nancy Island Museum, Wasaga Beach Provincial Park, Box 183, Wasaga Beach, Ontario B0S 1A0, tel (705) 429-2516. The musem features the remains of the 1789 schooner *Nancy*, a British supply ship in the War of 1812, set afire by the US Navy in 1814. A model of the *Nancy*, dioramas and displays are on view. Open May 24-Labor Day, 10-4. Admission free; parking $2.50 per vehicle.

Old Fort William, Vickers Heights Post Office, Thunder Bay, Ontario P0T 2Z0, tel (807) 577-8461. This 125-acre site with 42 historic buildings recreates the fur-trading life at the fort in 1815. Costumed workers represent a colorful assortment of merchants, Indian traders and voyagers, and they encourage visitors to participate in ongoing activities. Small craft such as birch bark canoes and flat-bottomed bateaux are in use at the park, and a 60-ton schooner has been built on the site by local shipwrights. Open year round, daily. Call for hours and admission rates which vary with the seasons.

Ontario Science Center, 770 Don Mills Rd., Don Mills, Ontario M3C 1T3, tel (416) 429-4423 or 4100. Maritime exhibits may be found in the Transportation Division and the Canadian Resources Section. The first contains a diorama of a shipyard and ship models. The Resources Section has a model of the *Gjøa*, the Norwegian vessel which first completed the Northwest Passage, dioramas and other models. Open year round, except Christmas, daily 10-6. Adults $3, Children $1, Seniors free.

Port Colborne Historical and Marine Museum, 280 Kin St., PO Box 572, Port Colborne, Ontario L3K 5X8, tel (416) 839-7604. Within the Museum's 8 buildings are exhibits on local history and the maritime activities of the town. The research room has photos and genealogical information. Open year round, daily 12-5. Admission is free.

RMS *Segwun*, PO Box 68, Gravenhurst, Ontario P0C 160, tel (705) 687-6667. The only surviving coal-fired steamship on Lake Muskoka, the *Segwun* of 1887 is fully restored and offers cruises of varying lengths, some with meals. In operation June to October. Call or write for complete schedule and rates.

PRINCE EDWARD ISLAND

Basin Head Fisheries Museum, PO Box 248, Souris, Prince Edward Island C0A 2B0, tel (402) 357-2966. Located in a former fishing port, this museum has a collection of regional small craft and fishing gear. Facilities include an old cannery with processing demonstrations and a small factory producing wooden packing crates for salt fish. Museum displays include models and dioramas illustrating fishing techniques and the variety of boats used. Open June-Sept. Call for hours and admission fees.

Green Park Shipbuilding Museum, Port Hill, Prince Edward Island C0B 2C0, tel (902) 831-2206. The Museum's Interpretive Center has a display on local shipbuilding in the 19th century. Located on the surrounding grounds are a Victorian home and small shipbuilding site complete with blacksmith and carpenter shops. Open mid-June to mid-Sept, daily 9-5. Adults $2.50, Seniors $1.25, Children under 12 free.

Cartier-Brébeuf National Historic Site, 175 de l'Espinay St., Quebec, Quebec G1K 7R3, tel (418) 648-4205. The site and its exhibits commemorate French explorer Jacques Cartier's first winter in Canada, his explorations, encounters with the Native Americans, and attempts at establishing a settlement. Centerpiece at the site is *La Grande Hermine*, a replica of Cartier's16th century caravel. Open year round; hours vary by the month. Admission free.

David M. Stewart Museum, The Old Fort (Vieux Fort), 20 chemin du Tour de l'Ile, Montréal, Quebec H3C 4G6, tel (514) 861-6701. Located on St. Helen's Island, the museum focuses on the European discovery, exploration and settlement of North America, specifically through the St. Lawrence seaway. Museum holdings include 22,000 objects of which 300 are maritime, and a library containing 6,000 documents. Permanent exhibits include a gallery of 18th century French prints, drawings and carvings, and a mid-18th century model of the *Jupiter*. Also of maritime interest are the collection of rare maps, scientific instruments and a 1688 Coronelli globe of the earth. Open year round, Wed-Mon 10-6. Call for admission rates.

Grosse Ile National Historic Site, 2 rue d'Auteuil, PO Box 2474, Quebec, Quebec G1K 7R3, tel (418) 648-4168. Situated in the upper St. Lawrence estuary, this island was the arrival point of hundreds of thousands of European immigrants. Guided tours are offered and excursions are available, but require reservations. Open June-Sept, Wed-Sun. Call for hours and rates.

Musée del la Mer, Inc., CP 69 Havre-Aubert, Iles de la Madeleine G0B 1J0, tel (418) 937-5711. Exhibits on seafaring, fishing, whaling and the history of Iles de la Madeleine are on view in a 7,000 sq ft-gallery. Ship models, maps, cannons and anchors enliven the displays, along with reproductions of a forge and a smoke house for fish. Open year round, Mon-Fri 9-6, Sat-Sun 10-6. Adults $2, Children $1.

Musée Maritime Bernier, 55 des Pienniers est, l'Islet-sur-Mer, Quebec G0R 2BO, tel (418) 247-5001. L'islet-sur-Mer, once a small shipbuilding center, dedicated a small chapel to townsmen lost at sea. That chapel now houses the library, archives and museum, which focuses on the St. Lawrence and local history. The Museum also owns three vessels: the wooden trading schooner *Jean-Yvan*, the icebreaker *Ernest Lapointe*, and the hydrofoil *Bras d'Or*. Open year round, daily 9-5; summer 9-8. Call for admission information.

Port of Quebec in the 19th Century, 100 rue St. André, Quebec, Quebec G1K 7R3, tel (418) 648-3300. An interpretive center located on the waterfront in the old port of Quebec, this museum illustrates the vital commercial role of the port, especially with regard to the lumber and shipbuilding trades. Four floors of exhibits include figures in period costume, models, illustrations, slide shows and sound tracks, all of which help recreate the dockside life of Quebec a century ago. Open year round, call for hours. Admission free.

AFTERWORD

To Research Maritime History
by Dave Hull
Principal Librarian, J. Porter Shaw Library
San Francisco Maritime National Historical Park

Maritime history is a crossroads of the disciplines; here intersects not only straightforward history, economics and ethnology, but also music, geography, naval architecture and engineering, art, law, literature and archaeology. As yet, academics rarely focus on maritime history, but because of its multifaceted nature, one can find significant maritime holdings in the great university libraries as well as the great public libraries. For example, to my amazement I once ran across a complete run of *Lloyds Register* on the shelves at UC Berkeley—available for circulation!

It may be seen then, that to do research in maritime history, one need not be near a library specializing in maritime history; to begin, go to your nearest large library and talk to the reference librarian, who will direct you to many sources, doubtless including Sheehy's *Guide to Reference Works*, a useful item along the lines of a bibliography of bibliographies. Even if they do not have what you need, they will have union lists that may identify what you do need and where it is; they can borrow it for you on interlibrary loan, a service available in virtually every library in the country. Dr. Samuel Johnson, who ought to know, declared: "Knowledge is of two sorts; one either knows a thing, or he knows where to find out a thing." It is a creed subscribed to by every librarian.

Libraries specializing in maritime history are usually attached to museums and range greatly in depth, focus, degree of access to information in the collections, and degree of access to the collections themselves. It may be fairly said that every institution has some collection of information, for where there is any intellectual activity, information will accumulate. All too often, for good reasons of course, that information is not professionally managed,* which means that it will not be catalogued or preserved. While research in these collections will take more "browsing," they are often open for research. For all museum libraries, it is advisable to call first for hours and availability of collections. A letter is usually better only if it is a reference inquiry (include your phone number), but because staffing is so limited, a personal visit (to do the research yourself) is most likely to produce the result you want.

Which library has what materials? It is safe to assume that museums will collect information relating to subjects in which they have significant artifactual holdings; a museum with a good collection of figureheads, for example, will probably have books on figureheads.

It is also safe to assume that most museums will collect information on their immediate locale, but also be aware that you may be able to find in any given location information ranging far afield. This happens for one of two reasons: in maritime history we deal with voyages—which have two ports, one of which may as well be on the other side of the world as down the river; the other reason has to do with opportunity and absence of a scope of collections statement— a (hypothetical) collection of information on Egyptian craft in an Ohio River museum, for example. For whatever reason information collections may be

---

*See Dave Hull and Henry Fearnley, "The Museum Library in the United States: A Sample," in *Special Libraries,* July 1976, pp. 289-299, a statistical profile of museum libraries. The economic information is dated, but this article is still valid today in its observations.

present, be open to the (obvious) fact that information is where you find it; in other words, look everywhere.

Having advanced that bewildering and possibly disconcerting prospect (a last-ditch approach), let me report that there are a number of organized approaches to information in maritime history.

Among published sources, information on maritime history is best outlined in Robert Albion's *Maritime and Naval History; an Annotated Bibliography* (fourth edition, 1972) and its supplement, and most detailed in the 15-volume Mariners Museum *Dictionary Catalog of the Library*. There are also subject-specific bibliographies, such as *The Hill Collection of Pacific Voyages*, and bibliographies in related subjects, such as *The Pacific Northwest; an index to people and places in books*. Really good guides and subject surveys, such as Norman Brouwer's *International Register of Historic Ships*, include bibliographical references. Periodical literature is significant and accessible through some of the more significant self-indexing periodicals such as *Mariner's Mirror* and *American Neptune* as well as through *Reader's Guide* and before that through *Poole's Index to Periodical Literature*. Newspaper stories are often the only contemporary account of an incident, and the two best historical indexes to US newspapers are available in *The New York Times Index* (coverage beginning in 1851) and the various microform publications of the California State Library (coverage of San Francisco newspapers, et al., beginning in the 1840s). I only scratch the surface of published sources, of course, but it serves to illustrate what research may be done at large general libraries.

Most of these sources would be available in at least the large specialized maritime history libraries. But there are also in these libraries the *unpublished* sources of information in maritime history, namely, their catalogues, their working indexes, the information floating around in brains waiting for the plucking or for serendipitous discovery.

What then are the published approaches to the libraries of maritime history? One can use any of the general guides to maritime museums, beginning, of course, with the one you are reading at this moment! Another easily obtainable listing would be the annual "Guide to the Naval & Nautical Museums of North America," published in the January issue of *Sea Classics*. Then there is Hartley Edward Howe's *North America's Maritime Museums: An Annotated Guide* (1987), which includes a subject index. This index can be a useful approach to find the library you need, by reference not only to the text, but also—now armed with museum names corresponding to desired subjects—to the *Official Museum Directory*, published by the American Association of Museums, which identifies when a given museum's facilities include a library as well as what that museum's research fields and collections are.

Then there are at least two guides which describe collections of information for specific aspects of maritime history. *Maritime Folklife Resources* (Library of Congress, 1980) lists 172 libraries, archives, museums and historical societies, but of particular value is its indexing of these collections by 26 subjects, such as "Mess equipment and utensils," "Belief systems and ritual," and "Recipes." And Mary Malloy's *African Americans in the Maritime Trades: A Guide to Resources in New England* (Kendall Whaling Museum, Sharon, Massachusetts, 1990) does just what its title suggests, in addition sporting a thorough bibliography.

These last two works are the type that make glad the hearts of reference librarians, for then we can intone authoritatively with Dr. Johnson: "Well, I'm sorry we don't have that information here, but I can tell you where you can find it."

INDEX OF MARITIME MUSEUMS AND VESSELS IN CANADA